History

History
TODAY

John Rogers—
sealed with blood

The story of the first Protestant
martyr of Mary Tudor's reign

Tim Shenton

DayOne

© Day One Publications 2007

First printed 2007

ISBN 978–1–84625–084–2

British Library Cataloguing in Publication Data available

Published by Day One Publications

Ryelands Road, Leominster, HR6 8NZ

☎ 01568 613 740 FAX 01568 611 473

email—sales@dayone.co.uk

web site—www.dayone.co.uk

North American—e-mail—sales@dayonebookstore.com

North American—web site—www.dayonebookstore.com

Cover design by Wayne McMaster

Designed by Steve Devane and printed by Gutenberg Press, Malta

Contents

Commendations

Tim Shenton has produced yet another well-documented, gripping biography of a real hero of faith—John Rogers (d. 1555), renowned biblical editor and first Marian martyr. Follow Rogers's fascinating career from Antwerp to Germany, and back again to England, where he was arrested, remained steadfast under intense interrogation, and paid the ultimate price for confessing Christ. This is a great book about an important epigone; hopefully, Rogers will no longer be marginalized! Highly recommended for teenagers and adults.

—Joel R. Beeke, Puritan Reformed Theological Seminary, Grand Rapids, Michigan

Shenton weaves a brilliant tapestry from original sources and introduces the reader to many compelling and complex personalities. Well-proportioned in its emphasis, this history will be a vital contribution to studies of Protestant martyrs in Queen Mary's reign.

—Randall J. Pederson, co-author of Meet the Puritans

Michael A.G. Haykin

The life of John Rogers (1500–1555) has been largely overlooked in recent Reformation scholarship. Understandably the achievements of William Tyndale and Thomas Cranmer have been central in these recent studies. Both of these men were superb scholars, passionate about the biblical Christianity then being rediscovered and imbued with a rich sense of the nature of genuine Christian catholicity. Rogers, though, was also an excellent scholar, as Tim Shenton shows in this fresh biography, and his publication of what is called the Matthew's Bible (1537)—so-named because of a pen-name used by Rogers—was a critical step in making the English people a 'people of the book'. Rogers's first edition of this Bible pioneered the use of marginal notes, which would be a key aspect of the English biblical tradition, enabling the unschooled person who could read access to Scripture commentary.

Rogers's life, though, also speaks of absolutes and ultimate values. He died as a martyr during the reign of Mary I for what he was right to view as biblical convictions. This aspect of Rogers's life occupies significant space in this new biography, and rightly so. Martyrdom, and theological reflection on it, are not prominent features of western Christian thought. But the Church is ever a Church of martyrs. Biblical Christianity stands for non-negotiables and rock-hard convictions, about which compromise is impossible, and as such, the world around the Church will vent its fury on her members for what it regards as intolerance and narrow-mindedness. That venting might take the form of ostracism and verbal abuse, but frequently it spills over into physical violence. And Rogers lived in a day when the latter was all too frequent. That such violence has ever been used by the Church against its opponents is utterly wrong—a fact that was the case in the Reformation era and that Shenton clearly acknowledges. But this should not be used as an excuse to avoid thinking about the Evangelical martyrs of that era and the meaning of their giving their lives for the love of the Lord Jesus and his holy truth. We in the west sorely need to craft a theology of martyrdom—it would put backbone into our proclamation and living and help us remember brothers and sisters going through fiery trials even today in other parts of the world. And remembering men like Rogers is a great help in the development of such a theology.

Foreword

How different then is his life, as detailed here by Shenton, from that of one of his main opponents, Bishop Stephen Gardiner, of whom it has been said, 'his life achieved little'. That cannot be said of Rogers, who, by divine grace, sealed his life's witness by his blood.

Michael Haykin
Principal and Professor of Church History and Reformed Spirituality, Toronto Baptist Seminary, Toronto, Ontario

I started to pen these words as I was sitting in a hotel restaurant just after the speeches of a wedding reception had finished. As I watched a group of Christian guests laughing and dancing to the music of a non-Christian band, with seemingly not a care in the world, I started to contrast in my own mind the Christianity of the twenty-first century, with its emphases on personal health and prosperity, with the Christianity that would have surrounded John Rogers in prison at Newgate or on his final march to the stake in Smithfield. Maybe such a contrast is not possible as the two generations are nearly 500 years apart and today's society is so very different to how it was in the sixteenth century; but, on the other hand, the gospel is the same in every generation and our faith in the unshakeable and immutable truth of Christ should be as strong now as it has ever been.

But as I sat watching the guests enjoying themselves, I wondered how many of us believe in Jesus Christ deeply enough to be ready to die for him if the hour called for it. Could we take off our dancing shoes and put away our lives of merriment to take that long and lonely walk to the scaffold or be willing to lay our head on the guillotine block?

Sometimes in the western world, as we consume so much of our time and energy in trying to find new ways of enjoying ourselves and in living a life of pleasure and ease, we forget that there are men and women and children in many different countries *at this very moment* who are facing that ultimatum of preparing themselves for death because of their faith in Jesus Christ.

As the dancers joked and pushed each other in fun, taking the odd respite to sip their beer or wine, I felt compelled to ask myself some serious questions. How deeply and firmly do I believe in Christ? Am I so embedded in him that nothing and no one will be able to uproot me? Is Jesus Christ so important to me that if, like John Rogers, I was threatened with imprisonment or death, I would be ready to take those steps down to the dungeon and to hold out my hands to the chains of my enemies? I suppose I shall never know until that dreaded day arrives when I am faced with the devilish cry: deny your Lord and Saviour Jesus Christ or face imprisonment or the firing squad.

John Rogers was not so much burnt at the stake because of his 'general' faith in Christ, but because of two particular doctrines he held that he thought were essential to that faith. He was prepared to die, not only for his Saviour, but for the truth about his Saviour. He held those doctrines so firmly that even when a host of enemies lined up against him he was unwilling to compromise or adapt his views to make them more palatable. Jesus once told his disciples that they must deny themselves, take up their cross daily and follow him, all the way to death if required. Are we ready to follow Jesus Christ in that way and to walk in the footsteps of a man like Rogers?

In our land today there is an ever-increasing likelihood that persecution of Christians is not far around the corner. While I am not wanting to be alarmist or scare-mongering, I do think the time is ripe for us to examine our faith, not just on a superficial level and according to our own thoughts and feelings, but in the light of God's word and the illumination of the Holy Spirit, to see first and foremost whether or not we *have a saving faith*. How terrible it would be if we were deluding ourselves into thinking that we were on the narrow road that leads to eternal life when in fact we were on the broad road to destruction! Secondly, we must ask ourselves: Is my faith built on the foundation of Christ and his apostles, a foundation that will not rock when shaken by the strong winds of persecution?

There is no one but Jesus Christ who is worth following and dying for. He is the Lord of heaven and earth, waiting with open arms to welcome his saints into eternal glory, just as he waited for Stephen, the first New Testament martyr, and for John Rogers, the first martyr in the reign of Queen Mary I. My prayer is that as you read about John Rogers, your faith might be strengthened to such a point that never again will it quiver as the storms rage around it.

I am indebted to Joseph Lemuel Chester and his book *John Rogers: the compiler of the first authorized English Bible, the pioneer of the English Reformation, and its first martyr*. His work is thorough and well investigated and his conclusions are mostly sound, although his repeated and often unjustified criticism of the martyrologist John Foxe is more than a little tiresome.

Inevitably many of the works I have studied for this book have been written in the sixteenth century. As far as possible I have tried to modernize the text; however, even after alteration some words and sentence constructions appear awkward by today's standards. In such cases my aim has been to clarify the meaning without changing too drastically the actual words spoken. I have worked from the premiss that it is more important to quote accurately than to interpret loosely. I have also consulted a number of modern works on the Tudor period.

I have deliberately avoided lengthy discussions about some aspects of Rogers's life and the somewhat tedious detail about his writings and translation work, for my aim has been to reach, inspire and inform readers rather than impress them with pretended scholarship.

Tim Shenton

John Rogers

Early career

It is hard to imagine the political upheavals and dangers that engulfed England during Rogers's life in the sixteenth century, and the almost dictatorial powers of the reigning monarch, especially when our own queen is virtually powerless politically. Think of the uproar and horror that would ensue if Elizabeth II made some of the murderous decisions that Henry VIII made with such impunity!

It is also hard to imagine how religion and politics could be so intertwined, when most politicians today, if they are not atheists, studiously avoid any mention of God or the Bible or morality. But then can we imagine anyone being in grave danger for translating the word of God into English, or publicly burned at the stake because he disagrees with certain doctrines of the Roman Catholic Church?

Sometimes one has to be reminded of the brutality and cheapness of life that then existed within England, or to travel to a place like Oxford and stand on the cross in the road that marks the spot where Nicholas Ridley and Hugh Latimer were burned to death in 1555. With imagination you can almost hear those immortal and prophetic words of Latimer's to his fellow sufferer: 'Be of good cheer, Master Ridley, and play the man. We shall this day light such a candle, by God's grace, in England, as I trust shall never be put out.' How sad it is, after all the martyrs endured, that today that light is in danger of being extinguished. May God once again raise men to preach the truth without compromise or fear so that Latimer's candle, by God's grace, will never be put out.

Birth and education

John Rogers was born at the beginning of this century of upheaval, sometime between the years 1500 and 1505 at the village or hamlet of Deritend

The burning of Hugh Latimer and Nicholas Ridley

in the parish of Aston, then in the suburbs of Birmingham. During these years Henry VII's eldest son Arthur was being prepared for his royal future, which included his marriage to Catherine of Aragon in 1501, but Arthur died the following year, probably before the marriage was consummated. In 1503 Queen Elizabeth died and the king's attention was turned to protecting his surviving son, Prince Henry, whose accession was only a few years away.

Rogers's father by the same Christian name was engaged in the metal industry, making metal furniture for horse harnesses. He was evidently a wealthy man. He married Margery Wyatt and they had five children: John, William, Edward, Ellenor and Joan. Their eldest, John, was educated at Pembroke Hall, Cambridge, where he graduated BA in 1526. This was the same college at which Nicholas Ridley was a member and it is likely that Rogers was not only his contemporary, but acquainted with him as well. The preaching of Hugh Latimer was also beginning to make a stir in Cambridge about this time and there is little doubt that it exercised considerable influence on the mind of Rogers at a later period.

Although there is no record of whether or not Rogers distinguished himself as a scholar at the university, he was obviously a hardworking student, setting good standards of discipline and preparing himself for the great task of editing and translating the Bible in which he was soon to be engaged and after which he was to be regarded as one of the first scholars of the age.

Holy orders

In the same year as he took his degree it is noted by some that he was chosen to the Cardinal's (now Christ's) College at Oxford and made a junior canon; but this is unlikely due to his age. Cardinal Wolsey formally opened Cardinal's College in 1526. The college buildings took over the site of St Frideswide's Monastery, suppressed by Wolsey to fund his college, which became a favourite with him. At that time many efforts were made to attract to it the most noted and promising scholars from other institutions (the misinformation of Rogers's transfer probably stems from these efforts). Large inducements were offered so that its reputation might be rapidly established and its interests advanced. Unknown to Wolsey, several of the young graduates that he brought from Cambridge had already imbibed the Reformed teaching, which they soon began to spread among the Oxford students. 'Thus the college, which Wolsey had gone to such trouble to establish, immediately became a focal point for the spreading of "Lutheran heresy", even though he himself was opposed to such teachings.'

Rogers went into holy orders and for nearly two years he officiated as rector of Holy Trinity the Less, Knightrider Street in London, so

St Mary Overie

named to distinguish it from Holy Trinity Priory Aldgate. He was presented to the living by the prior and convent of St Mary Overie in Southwark in the diocese of Winchester on 26 December 1532. He was canonically instituted in the same, with all its rights and appurtenances. He voluntarily resigned in the latter part of 1534, his successor being appointed on 24 October of that year. After his martyrdom his remains were brought back to Holy Trinity for burial. At this time Rogers was an orthodox Catholic priest.

The Merchant Adventurers

In 1534, the Merchant Adventurers, a commercial corporation, called Rogers to be chaplain to the English factory at Antwerp. The Fellowship, or Company, of Merchant Adventurers was formally created in 1486 and consisted of those London merchants who controlled the profitable cloth trade with Flanders, on which England's commercial prosperity largely depended. Throughout the 1530s, in spite of some early trouble with the Emperor, Charles V, ruler of Flanders, the Merchant Adventurers enjoyed a smooth and financially successful business. They were helped by the encouragement and policies of Thomas Cromwell, earl of Essex, who himself had been a merchant and had close connections with the Adventurers. Rogers served them for about three years as a quiet, unoffending priest, like many others of his class at that time.

From this appointment it is clear that Rogers did not leave England from motives of personal safety, although it is probable that his faith in the Roman Catholic Church had already been shaken; for he intimated to Stephen Gardiner, the Lord Chancellor, during his preliminary examination before the Privy Council (22 January 1555), a week before his final trial and examination, that Gardiner and the other bishops first brought him to the knowledge of the *pretended* primacy of the Bishop of Rome *twenty years* before, when he was a young man. It may therefore be reasonable to assume that he resigned his rectorship of Holy Trinity the Less on account of his changing sentiments and gladly accepted the invitation to the Adventurers, knowing that at Antwerp he could enjoy greater freedom of conscience than was then tolerated in England.

The Reformation advances

During the ten years from Rogers's graduation, the Reformation in Europe steadily advanced. It spread to Sweden and Denmark, established itself in Bern and became official in Basel. The second Protestant university was founded at Marburg (the oldest Protestant university existed from 1526 to 1530 in Liegnitz in Silesia) and the goal of the institution was to educate 'learned, able, and God-fearing persons, preachers and officials for Christian benefit and the good of the

Martin Luther

common land'. In 1534, Henry VIII, who had acceded to the throne in 1509, was declared supreme head of the Church of England, thus signalling the final break with Rome and the jurisdiction of the Pope, whose authority had been under attack in England for about a year.

Furthermore, Luther was declared an outlaw and therefore could not attend the Diet at Augsburg (1530); he also finished his German translation of the Bible. Philip Melanchthon's *Augsburg Confession*, a statement of Lutheran beliefs, was presented to Charles V on 25 June at the Diet. John Calvin started the Protestant movement in France and published his first work, a commentary on Seneca's *De Clementia* (1532). Tyndale finished printing the New Testament (1526), which was the first printing of the New Testament in English and the first translation of the Scriptures from the Biblical Greek. Smuggled copies of this work were soon circulated throughout England. Four years later Tyndale's translation of the Pentateuch also appeared in England, with a prologue headed 'WT to the Reader', and later the book of Jonah and his exposition of the first epistle of John. In 1534 his revised New Testament was printed and in the spring of the following year he was living contentedly at Thomas Poyntz's English merchants' boarding house in Antwerp.

Opposition

However, there was considerable opposition to the Reformation. Cardinal Wolsey presided over a huge burning of 'Lutheran' books at St Paul's Cathedral, and Bishop Cuthbert Tunstall worked out a deal with a London merchant, Augustine Packington, who had connections with the Christian Brethren in Germany, to buy up all copies of Tyndale's New Testament right off the 'pirate' press of Christopher Van Endhoven in order to burn them. Thomas Bilney, a respected Cambridge preacher and 'Lutheran sympathizer', was dragged from his pulpit, imprisoned and then burned at the stake (1531), followed a couple of years later by Tyndale's good friend John Frith.

Thomas Bilney led away in chains

Conversion and marriage

While in Antwerp, Rogers became acquainted with William Tyndale, who had escaped from England in 1524, after realizing that there was no place of safety left in that country to translate the New Testament. He had initially travelled to Germany and then later on to Antwerp. While talking with Tyndale and other godly men about the Scriptures, Rogers grew in his knowledge of the gospel of God to such an extent that he gradually cast off the 'heavy yoke of Popery', perceiving it to be impure and idolatrous. However, it was probably not until he closely examined the Bible in preparation for its publication, some time after Tyndale's death, that he finally and fully turned his back on Roman Catholicism. He then found it necessary to find a new home in a less bigoted part of the country.

William Tyndale

Rogers was good friends with Tyndale until the latter's martyrdom early in October 1536. It is not surprising, however, that Tyndale makes no mention of Rogers in his writings or correspondence, thinking that someone who was not yet confirmed in the new faith might be personally injured if his inclination to change his creed was voiced abroad.

Marriage

The most important personal event that took place in the life of Rogers at this time was his marriage, an event that could not have taken place until his separation from the Catholic Church. With the biblical understanding that matrimony is both honest and honourable, he determined to disregard the canon of his church, which stipulated that he was prohibited from marrying, under certain penalties. He therefore found a wife, and released himself from any allegiance or connection with 'his old views'. It was the end of that gradual change in his views and faith and the beginning of an open warfare between him and his former associates.

The marriage must have taken place in the latter part of 1536 or early in 1537, the same year as the publication of Matthew's Bible, although a private ceremony may have taken place earlier as, after some eleven years of marriage (in the spring of 1548), they brought eight children from Germany to England. After his condemnation on 29 January 1555, Rogers declared to the Lord Chancellor, when appealing to him that his wife might visit him, that she had been married to him for eighteen years, making the date 1537. The name of his Protestant wife was Adriana de Weyden (meaning 'meadows'), anglicised into Pratt, who was from an Antwerp family. She was the daughter of his printer Jacob van Meteren, who had been the sponsor behind the printing of Miles Coverdale's English Bible of 1535, and has been described as 'more richly endowed with virtue and soberness of life than with worldly treasures'.

Wittenberg

After six years in Antwerp, Rogers travelled with his new wife to Wittenberg in Germany, where he matriculated on 25 November 1540, and where twenty years before Luther's manifesto had inaugurated the Reformation. He probably moved there so he could be nearer Luther and Melanchthon and other kindred spirits of the Reformation, as well as for safety reasons, for although the Merchant Adventurers at Antwerp gave shelter and encouragement to the first Reformers, their protection in an emergency could not be fully trusted, especially as Tyndale had been captured in their midst. Rogers's connection with the new translation of the Bible, his marriage and his rejection of Popery had by then, to some extent at least, become public knowledge. He was surrounded by enemies and therefore had to escape the scene of his conversion and the place where he had committed the offences so odious to the Catholics.

In Wittenberg, through indefatigable study and application, he increased in godly learning and soon spoke German well. He became one of the four superintendents of the Lutheran church in the Dietmarsh region of northwest Germany. With Melanchthon's support, he accepted the challenging pastorate at Meldorf. Back in 1524, Henry of Zutphen had been lynched by a drunken mob in that district, the alcohol being provided by local monks. He struggled for a time with the regional accent and Melanchthon advised him that pronunciation problems would only be overcome in time.

VIVENTIS·POTVIT·DVRERIVS·ORA·PHILIPPI
MENTEM·NON·POTVIT·PINGERE·DOCTA
MANVS
1526

Philip Melanchthon

For four and a half years Rogers lived an unobtrusive life in Meldorf. About a year before he left he led an initiative by local clergy to try to reduce the number of murders that were occurring in the region. The inhabitants were confused about self-defence and unhappy that murderers could buy their way out of the death penalty. The ministers threatened to stop preaching and administering the sacrament if the secular authorities did not enforce imperial laws against murderers. Rogers, in the only letter of his that survives (written from Meldorf), comes out in support of those who think that only murderers deserve to be put to death, which is an interesting opinion for Rogers to hold in view of what happened with Joan of Kent (see chapter 8).

At Meldorf he fulfilled the practical duties of his calling, served God in his public ministrations, enjoyed a happy relationship with his wife, and a close association with German scholars and Reformers. During this time of peace he was being prepared and disciplined for the fierce battles and fiery trials that lay ahead. About the spring of 1548, after Edward VI's enthronement the year before, he left Meldorf, to the evident grief of his people, and returned with his family to England.

The Matthew's Bible

David Daniell, in his magisterial work *The Bible in English*, says about Rogers: 'To this steadfast and courageous reformed pastor and preacher the English-speaking Christian world owes a debt of particular gratitude. Working with, apparently, the printer Matthew Crom in Antwerp, John Rogers put together in 1537 a handsome thick folio [of a large complete Bible], well printed in clear black letter in double columns.'

William Tyndale and Rogers

William Tyndale, who had published his translation of the New Testament in 1526 and that of the Pentateuch in 1530, earnestly desired to complete the whole Bible. There is no positive proof of Rogers's initial involvement although their friendship suggests that he helped when and where he could and that he had some knowledge of the character and condition of the work (he was probably a scholar of the Greek New Testament and he had a good grasp of Hebrew and Aramaic). If this had not been the case, Rogers would not have been so ready to take up and complete the unfinished manuscript after Tyndale's arrest. Rogers arrived in Antwerp late in 1534 and Tyndale was arrested in May 1535, so their personal association could not have lasted more than a few months. Nevertheless, it would not have taken long for both men to form a common bond.

It is not hard to imagine the two men sitting in Tyndale's study in the house of Thomas Poyntz, discussing the Scriptures and encouraging one another in the faith; and then busily engaged in translating the Bible into their own language. In all probability both men failed to realize the greatness of their mission and the effect their work would have on the future of the church.

Thomas Poyntz

Thomas Poyntz, in whose house Tyndale and probably Rogers lived, was a wealthy merchant and described as a 'good, shrewd friend and loyal sympathizer'. He was the brother of Lady Anne Walsh of Little Sodbury and the head of the Merchant Adventurers' house in Antwerp; it was there that he sheltered Tyndale as his sister had in England. John Foxe's 1563 biography of Tyndale concludes with an account probably written by Thomas Poyntz, and received from him or someone close to him.

When Tyndale was arrested, on or near 21 May 1535, the procurer-general, Pierre Dufief, immediately raided Poyntz's house and confiscated all Tyndale's property, including his books and papers. However, the Old Testament historical books in English were probably safely with Rogers. Tyndale was taken to the castle of Vilvorde outside Brussels, where he was imprisoned for the next sixteen months.

Poyntz did all he could to help. He wrote to his brother John at the English court, saying that the king never had 'a truer hearted subject to his grace' than Tyndale. 'The king's grace should have of him at this day as high a treasure as of any man living … there be not many perfecter men this day

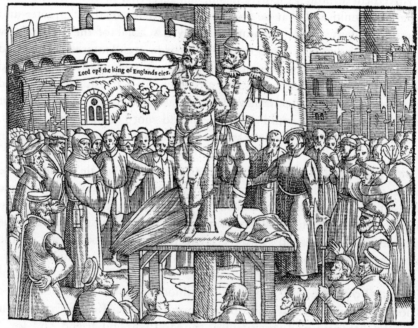

The execution of William Tyndale

living, as knows God.' Initially it seemed as though Poyntz's efforts had succeeded for he was told at Brussels that Tyndale would be released to him. Henry Phillips, who had betrayed Tyndale for cash, fearing that his reward was under threat, announced to the authorities that Poyntz was 'a dweller in the town of Antwerp, and there had been a succourer of Tyndale, and was one of the same opinion'. The procurer-general arrested Poyntz and imprisoned him. He was kept under house arrest in Brussels while a case was built up against him. The procurer-general spent five or six days examining him on more than 100 articles, before drawing up about twenty-four against him, which were passed on to the commissioners, who then appeared every eight days to continue the prosecution and to hear Poyntz's defence, which was hampered by restrictions placed on him. This went on from the beginning of November to the end of January.

After being held in Brussels for some twelve or thirteen weeks, Poyntz realized he would be put to death, and on the night he was to be transferred to a stronger prison, he escaped and at dawn slipped out of Brussels. Horsemen were sent after him, but he knew the land and made it to England. His wife refused to join him. He was banished from the Netherlands and his business and domestic arrangements collapsed and never recovered. In 1547, twelve years later, on his brother's death, he succeeded to the ancestral manor of North Ockenden, but was too poor to live there. He died in 1562 and was buried at St Dunstan's in London, despite the fact his family home was in Essex.

Rogers takes up Tyndale's manuscripts

At Tyndale's arrest it was not known where his bulky manuscript translation of Joshua to 2 Chronicles was located. He could not have passed on that information at the time of or after his arrest because that event occurred unexpectedly through the treachery of Phillips and he was not allowed to enjoy any conversation with his former acquaintances during his imprisonment. Somehow the manuscript survived the illegal raid on Poyntz's house and in all likelihood was in the possession of Rogers, who made sure it was printed in what became 'the most influential of all the early printed English Bibles', the Matthew's Bible.

The frontispiece to the Matthew's Bible

If Rogers was not personally involved in the work at the time of Tyndale's arrest, it is certain he started his labours immediately after that event or how else could he have completed the work ready for the publication of the entire volume in 1537? No doubt, from his own inclination and the encouragement of Tyndale's friends, he took up the manuscript, and while ministering to his congregation, devoted his spare time to the Matthew's Bible.

David Daniell thinks that Rogers was an ideal person to take Tyndale's work further. 'He was a graduate with an undoubted flair for language' and 'it is likely that he was already a scholar of the Greek New Testament.' In the Matthew's Bible 'we can see his grasp of Hebrew and Aramaic, versions of the Old Testament in Greek and Latin, and his use of recent European work on the Scriptures as well as his knowledge of the Fathers. His understanding of the religious needs of ordinary people, of the ploughboys of the Dietmarsh region, was one with his later power as a London preacher.'

The Matthew's Bible, 1537

The translation and the publishers

A large portion of the Old Testament, extending to the beginning of Isaiah had been finished and printed before the subsequent publishers, Richard Grafton and Edward Whitchurch, two citizens of London, became involved in the undertaking. This had been accomplished through the private subscriptions of Tyndale's friends, most probably the English Merchants at Antwerp. Grafton and Whitchurch learned in some way that this translation was already well advanced. They hurried to Antwerp to see what terms could be arranged with those involved and almost at once agreed to be the future proprietors, underwriting an edition of 1500 copies, which were shipped to England. Grafton was so confident of the financial success of this venture that he put into it almost his entire fortune.

All the books so far had been supervised by Rogers and printed, for at this point in the Matthew's Bible a new numbering starts and a title page is inserted with the words 'The prophetes in Englishe', on the reverse of which, above and below a large woodcut, are the initials RG and EW (Richard Grafton and Edward Whitchurch), indicating the point at which the new proprietors became involved with the work. They purchased the sheets already printed and employed Rogers to prepare and complete the remainder.

Richard Grafton

Richard Grafton was the son of a Shrewsbury skinner. His grandfather had been a chaplain at court to Edward V and then to Prince Arthur Tudor. He raised his grandson and apprenticed him to the prominent Cheapside grocer John Blagge, whose customers included Thomas Cranmer and Thomas Cromwell. Richard Grafton was admitted Freeman of the Company of Grocers in 1534. He soon met and befriended a member of the Haberdashers' Company, Edward Whitchurch.

After the Matthew's Bible both men concentrated their efforts on the folio Bible, known as 'the Great Bible' (1539), which was a revision of the Matthew's Bible but without the marginal notes, which, because of their Protestant bias, caused difficulties for some senior English clergy, who were still 'nervous about allowing the laity to read the Bible in English', especially if the notes led to it being read in a radically Protestant manner. In some ways the notes in the Matthew's Bible were published too early in the Reformation to make it the favoured choice for use in the churches.

Seven other editions of 'the Great Bible' were published before December 1541, and five separate editions of the New Testament of Rogers's version were printed during that time, in addition to several by other hands. Soon after Thomas Cromwell's fall (1540), Grafton was confined in Fleet prison for six weeks having printed a 'ballad' in Cromwell's praise, but he soon regained royal favour and became known as 'the king's printer' throughout the reign of Edward VI.

Grafton printed the first book of Homilies in 1547 and the first Book of Common Prayer two years later. On the accession of Lady Jane Grey he printed her proclamation, for which Queen Mary deprived him of the office of royal printer. After enduring a few more weeks' imprisonment he made peace with Mary but was not restored to his former position. After he retired from business as a printer, he was elected a member of parliament on several occasions, was twice warder of the Grocers' Company, and became a master of Bridewell Hospital, founded in 1553 by King Edward.

In spite of his efforts to obtain wealth it appears he was reduced to extreme poverty in later life, and after 1570 he proposed to become a public informer in order to benefit from the fines attached to the infraction of certain statutes concerning the cloth workers. He died about 1572. He is perhaps best known as a chronicler.

Edward Whitchurch

Grafton's right-hand man in many of his undertakings, Edward Whitchurch, was also a grocer, who accepted with enthusiasm the doctrines of the Reformation. He too was confined to prison for six weeks for printing unlawful books. Both Whitchurch and Grafton received jointly an exclusive patent for printing church service books and an exclusive right to print primers in Latin and English. In Edward's reign Whitchurch was on terms of intimacy with Protestant leaders and his press was always busy. He reprinted an edition of the New Testament in small octavo, many editions of the Prayer Book, and 'the Great Bible' in small folio.

In 1548 Rogers was with Edward Whitchurch at his house in Fleet Street and the little volume he produced bears on the title page their combined monogram, but Whitchurch was the sole publisher. On the accession of Mary he probably fled to Germany, but resumed business in London during the reign of Elizabeth, publishing a new edition of Thomas Phaer's *Regiment of Life* in 1560. It was his last undertaking. He married the widow of Thomas Cranmer, Margaret, and died in 1562, being buried at Camberwell.

The translated manuscripts of the Matthew's Bible

It is customary to attribute the Pentateuch and New Testament to Tyndale with minor variations (the latter from the so-called final 'GH' revision of his 1534 version). The books of the Old Testament from Ezra to Malachi (including Jonah) are taken from Coverdale with some significant changes, as also is the Apocrypha; but the historical books of the Old Testament from Joshua to 2 Chronicles are very different from Coverdale. It is now known that the English translation from the Hebrew of the nine historical books ending at 2 Chronicles is the work of Tyndale.

Rogers's work

On his arrest Tyndale left certain finished and unfinished manuscripts, being complete or incomplete translations of various parts of the Old Testament, with copious notes, all of which were in the possession of Rogers and to which he confined himself. Grafton, who wanted a speedy return for his outlay, urged him to finish the work as quickly as possible. In his haste Rogers used the manuscripts of Tyndale as far as he could and then, to satisfy the demands of his new employers, supplied the deficiencies from the published translation of Coverdale, which he corrected and altered as far as time would allow. All of this amounted to a huge volume of work for Rogers to have completed in such a short space of time, especially as Tyndale had not prepared him for the task before his capture.

The entire volume was printed in Antwerp apparently at the press of Matthew Crom, the latter part of July 1537, which means Rogers was only engaged on the project for a little more than two years. He was never keen to adopt Coverdale's version without making many and considerable alterations, omissions and additions in the portions of the Matthew's Bible attributed to him. He supplied his own translation for the short prayer of Manasseh in the Apocrypha, which Coverdale had omitted. For Job and Isaiah he used the commentaries of Oecolampadius and even translated afresh the opening chapters of Job, making them more coherent, which Coverdale had not done well. Nor did he follow Coverdale's arrangement very closely and, in one example, rejected three verses not found in the Hebrew that Coverdale had inserted into the fourteenth Psalm.

He took Tyndale's Pentateuch and New Testament and, after making some 330 changes to the former, made them accessible to a 'more influential English readership'.

All this means that it was thanks to John Rogers that these valuable manuscripts were not scattered to the four winds. The responsibility of completing the work was placed at his feet and he rose to the challenge with determination and courage. He placed the text in a complete state, probably comparing every verse with the original, added marginal illustrations, prefaces and other articles, which he prefixed to the whole work. In all he 'guarantee[d] that Tyndale was the maker of most of the English Bible for centuries to come'. Or to put it another way: as Rogers's labours were largely used in the preparation of 'the Great Bible', on which was based the Bishop's Bible, which in turn was the main foundation of the Authorized Version of 1611, 'Rogers may be credited with having effectively aided in the production of the classical English translation of the Bible'.

Rogers's notes

Interestingly, Stephen Gardiner, who always bitterly opposed the English version of the Bible, regarding any departure from the Scripture's 'original' Latin as heresy, addressed Rogers as 'Thomas Matthew' during his trial. He was not so much opposed to the preacher Rogers as to the translator Matthew, for he was astute enough to foresee that the English version was a serious threat to his church and religion.

The marginal notes alone are copious. From the texts of the French Bibles of Lefèvre (1530 and 1534, both printed in Antwerp by Martin de Keyser) and Olivétan (1535), and from his own knowledge, he greatly expanded the marginal notes in both Testaments. In Tyndale's Pentateuch he omitted three or four of the original marginal comments against the Pope and inserted his own notes from Pellican's Latin commentary. He supplied marginal notes to Tyndale's historical books and New Testament from the French Bibles, which meant that the whole volume had over 2000 marginal notes, excluding cross-references. His notes were pioneer work in Protestant glossing in English.

It may also be said that the Catholic clergy regarded his notes and prefaces as even more dangerous than the text itself. In the list of books prohibited in 1542, as appears in the official register of Bonner, they are particularly specified and especially described as of 'Thomas Matthew's doing'. However, as Martin Holt Dotterweich points out, 'while Tyndale and Rogers [in the Matthew's Bible] especially have been accused of writing polemical notes, a reading of their margins displays few such annotations; rather, the notes consist primarily of lexical explanation or comparison of a difficult passage to others which explain it, albeit with an identifiably Protestant slant'.

In the words of David Daniell, 'John Rogers needs more recognition for his contribution to marginal elucidation. Like Tyndale, his scholarship was at the ploughboy's disposal. He was able to refer the reader to the "Chaldee", the Aramaic version of the Old Testament, commonly called the Targum, and to the Greek Septuagint version, to elucidate Hebrew obscurities. He also took from the French versions chapter summaries throughout the whole Bible. Remembered by few now, sometimes only for his reading of the Hebrew "hallelujah" as "Praise the Everlasting", John Rogers, though neglected today, was a modern Biblical scholar.'

In 1549 John Day, John Foxe's friend and printer, and others published several editions of the Bible and New Testament in which they revised the marginal notes of the 1537 edition and described them as the notes of Thomas Matthew, who by then most people knew to be John Rogers.

A closer look at the Matthew's Bible

One of the remarkable features of the Matthew's Bible is the whole-page frontispiece depicting Adam and Eve enjoying Paradise before the Fall. In contrast to the usual depiction of the serpent tempting Eve to take the forbidden fruit, the first couple, naked yet unashamed, are surrounded by plants, animals and heavenly bodies in a beautiful landscape of lakes and hills, with a loving Creator watching over them. Eve smiles as monkeys play in a nearby tree, and Adam relaxes. The picture is one of peace and tranquillity. There is no sign of the serpent. These wood engravings were struck from blocks that had been used in a Dutch Bible printed at Lubeck in 1533.

The Bible itself comprises of 1,110 large folio pages, thick and heavy, with the text in strong black letters in two columns. The size of the volume is 30·2cm by 21·5cm, which is a little smaller than 'the Great Bible'. The books have ornamental openings and the pages have large print summary headings. Chapters are fully demarcated with summaries before the chapter titles and large upper case section letters in the outer margins. There are marginal notes, cross-references to other books of the Bible, explanatory notes, hands pointing to key passages and a few subheadings.

The volume opens with twenty preliminary pages (based on the French Bibles of Lefèvre and Olivétan), including the church calendar and an almanack for the years 1528–1557; summaries of the content of the Bible, which run like a religious encyclopaedia, taken verbatim from the French Bible translated by Pierre-Robert Olivétan and printed at Neuchâtel in 1535; and a brief account of world history from the creation to 1537. The order of the New Testament books follows the early Lutheran practice of placing Hebrews, James, Jude and Revelation at the end of the New Testament, in a category of their own, which reflected Luther's personal doubts concerning their canonicity—doubts not shared by other Reformers such as John Calvin or by Catholic opponents of the Reformation.

Title page

The language of the title page is very simple: *The Bible, which is all the Holy Scriptures: in which are contained the Old and New Testaments, truly and purely translated into English by Thomas Matthew, MDXXXVII. Set forth with the king's most gracious licence.* It was probably Grafton who wanted a name put to the translation, especially to the dedication to the king. Tyndale, who had the greatest claim to the work, was dead and his name was still odious to the Catholics. Rogers, who had a right to the distinction, probably refused the honour and so a fictitious name was used as a compromise. Perhaps Rogers chose two of his favourite Bible characters as a suitable pseudonym under which the book was to make its appearance. There is no truth in the suggestion that a real Thomas Matthew, a Lutheran fishmonger from Colchester, who might have been in Antwerp in 1536 and 1537, put together this scholarly tome.

Dedication to the king

The dedication to the king occupies three pages and opens with the words: 'To the most noble and gracious Prince King Henry the eight.' It is signed 'Your grace's faithful and true subject Thomas Matthew', with the initials HR (Henricus Rex) at the foot. Rogers recognized Henry VIII as his temporal master and as the supreme head of the church and addressed him with the dignity worthy of a sovereign. On the one hand, Rogers did not forget that he was a subject; and on the other, he wrote as a minister of the word of God, which he presented for the king's acceptance. In the way he wrote he felt confident that the Bible would be favourably received and that the 'Defender of the Faith' would exert his authority on its behalf. In reality he preached a 'hidden' sermon to the king, which appears to have been graciously received by that monarch.

In the course of his dedication, he wrote,

Now in as much as the Lord has raised you up before other princes in our time ... to attempt the things that do not a little unveil God's glory and had also opened your eyes to see the falsehood of the subtle and the innocency of the godly; to note the wiles of the children of this world and the simplicity of the holy, to abolish enormous and filthy abuses and in their stead to root and fix the right, true and perfect doctrine of

Henry VIII

Christianity. There is found no man to whom the transaction of the Lord's law can so worthily be offered and dedicated as to your most gracious highness. For I nothing mistrust but that it shall most acceptably come into your most favourable and sure protection ... It is no vulgar or common thing that is offered into your grace's protection, but the blessed word of God, which is everlasting and cannot fail, though heaven and earth should perish. So precious a thing requires a singular good patron and defender and finds no other to whom the defence thereof may so justly be committed as to your grace's majesty. It is the law of the celestial King, who rules all things ... and yet is it sometimes greatly furthered or hindered by the aid and hindrance of earthly and worldly princes...

But for the fortunate and prosperous estate of this our time (so far as concerns this your grace's realm) our high and unceasable thanks be given to the Lord of lords, who has dealt so mercifully with the inhabitants thereof, as to send them a prince that continually studies to see them enriched in all points of true godliness ...

Your grace's wisdom, illuminated of God, shall (we trust) so firmly establish the trade of godliness in your life time, that it shall nevertheless flourish after your decease... The everlasting Lord ... so stretch out his mighty hand and work so strongly in you that no storm of false prophets (the very destroyers of princes and realms) may hereafter be able to extinguish the light, which now in your grace's days has gone to shine; and double to you the addition of years that was given to Hezekiah, over and above those that you should normally live, that you may the better accomplish your most godly intent; and pour such streams of grace into your breast, that your persevering to the end may leave behind you this testimony of glory: that you have truly defended the pure faith of Christ, maintained his holy word, suppressed superstition, deleted and put away idolatry, ended the blasphemy of false prophets and brought your realm to the true trade of godliness; and bless you at this present with a son, by your most gracious wife Queen Jane [Seymour, whom the king had married on 30 May 1536; she died on 24 October 1537], who may prosperously and fortunately reign, and follow the godly steps of his father.

Although this dedication may appear today as excessively servile, it was the norm in those days to write in an elaborate and flattering style, especially if you wanted the recipient to grant a favour or to support your cause.

The Sum and Contents of all the Holy Scriptures

Two further articles were written by Rogers, the first he called *The Sum and Contents of all the Holy Scriptures, both of the Old and New Testaments*. It covers a brief but comprehensive synopsis of the doctrines of the Bible and, although written in the obscure and pedantic style of the day, can properly be called the sum of Christianity as it includes every important doctrine of the Christian religion. The opening paragraph reads:

First, the holy writings of the Bible teach us that there is one God, almighty, that had neither beginning nor ending; which of his own goodness did create all things; of whom all things proceed, and without whom there is nothing; which is righteous and merciful, and which works all things in all after his will; of whom it may not be demanded why he does this or that.

Later in the article he speaks of Christ and his saving work, saying,

In the New Testament, therefore, it is most evidently declared that Jesus Christ the true lamb and host, is come to us to reconcile us to the Father, paying on the cross the punishment due to our sins, and to deliver us from the bondage of the devil (to whom we served through sin) and to make us the sons of God, since he has given us the true peace and tranquillity of conscience, that we no longer do fear the pains of hell, which fear is put away by our faith, confidence and assurance that the Father gives us, drawing us into his Son...

To whom we must come and follow him with a cheerful heart, that he may instruct and teach us, for he is our master, meek and humble of heart; he is our example of whom we must learn the rule of good living. Further, he is our priest, the bishop and only mediator, who now sits on the right hand of God the Father, is our advocate and prays ever for us...

This is that Christ Jesus, which after he has killed the man of sin with the breath of his mouth, shall sit in his majesty and judge all men, giving to every one the works of his body, according to that he has done, whether it be good or bad.

He closed the article by saying that all are accursed who preach any other faith or salvation than only by Jesus Christ.

An Exhortation to the Study of the Holy Scriptures

The second article is *An Exhortation to the Study of the Holy Scriptures, gathered out of the Bible* and is only a page long. It is composed exclusively of verses selected from various parts of the Bible, consecutively and judiciously arranged. One example is taken from Proverbs 30:5–6: 'All the word of God is pure and clean; it is a shield to them that put their trust in it. Put nothing to his words, lest he reprove you and you be found a liar.' At the bottom are the large capital initials IR (John Rogers), which is the only occasion in the volume that Rogers personally appears.

A Table of Common Places

In order to awaken interest in the Bible and to make it more accessible to the ordinary person, Rogers prepared and arranged what he called *A Table of the Principal Matters contained in the Bible, in which the Readers may find and practise many Common Places.* He made a selection of important words and subjects most likely to interest the reader, arranged them alphabetically and appended to them references to appropriate passages of Scripture, with an explanation of their meaning, 'for the consolation of those who are not yet exercised and instructed in the holy Scripture. In the which are many hard places, as well of the Old as of the New Testament expounded, gathered together, concorded and compared one with another, so that the prudent reader (by the Spirit of God) may carry away pure and clear understanding. Whereby every man (as he is bound) may be made ready, strong and garnished to answer to all them that ask him a reason of his faith. This is also profitable for the particular and general exhortations which we make to certain persons or common people; and for to answer truly to heretics and to confound the adversaries of the word of God… the intention that none be deprived of so precious a treasure, the which you shall use to the honour and glory of God and to the edifying of his church.'

The *Table* stretches to twenty-six folio pages and is a dictionary, concordance and commentary all rolled into one. It highlights certain words, phrases, sentiments and doctrines, defines and explains them, and refers the reader to the proper texts for their support and defence. Every line and sentence is a starting point from which the reader can easily pursue his investigations and readily establish the doctrine involved, in order to confirm his own faith or that of others.

Heresies refuted

Rogers obviously had in mind to direct particular attention to those parts of the Bible which were in plain opposition to the doctrines of the Roman Catholic Church, for they are prominent throughout the work, especially in reference to the mass, the real presence and the marriage of priests. He was helped in this task by the previous labours of German editors.

It was imperative, for the strengthening of the Reformation, that these heresies were firmly and biblically refuted. It was not enough simply to place an English Bible before the people of England; their attention needed to be directed to those portions of it that were in direct conflict with the teachings of the priests. In this way the reader could satisfy his own mind in reference to the real doctrines of God on these points. He was also provided with the ready means of confuting his ordinary opponent and even the priests themselves. In its day, the *Table* was an invaluable tool for the establishment of the doctrines of the kingdom of God. Rogers, therefore, was the author of the first general English commentary on the Bible and the author of the first English concordance, and thus led the way for many to follow him.

When Gardiner and his followers realized it was useless to contend against the introduction of the English Bible, they turned their attention to Rogers's *Marginal Notes*, *Table of Common Places* and the *Prologues* by Tyndale, doing all in their power to curtail the spread of these 'dangerous additions'.

The Apocrypha

It is to be regretted that Rogers retained the books of the Apocrypha in the edition of the Bible he superintended. It seems likely that this matter was out of his control and that the publishers included the books. This conclusion is apparently correct because his notes, which are to be found everywhere else, appear nowhere in the Apocrypha; and his *Address to the Reader*, prefacing the Apocryphal books, is a distinct and positive protest against their inspiration. The translation is Coverdale's and Rogers left it without alteration, only adding a slight formal synopsis to each chapter and a translation of the prayer of Manasseh. On the last page of the Old Testament, before the Apocrypha, are the elaborate initials WT (William Tyndale).

Later editions

A second folio edition of the Matthew's Bible appeared in 1538 and Robert Redman is credited with having produced an edition in five volumes in 1540, but nothing further is known about this copy. It was twice reprinted in 1549, first by Thomas Raynalde and William Hill, and then by John Day and William Seres, with notes by Edmund Becke. Nicholas Hyll printed another edition in 1551.

The Bible's advance

A letter from Cranmer to Cromwell

Thomas Cranmer

The Matthew's Bible reached England in July 1537 and one of the first to receive a copy from Grafton was Archbishop Cranmer, who in turn sent it to Lord Cromwell, Henry's vicegerent for ecclesiastical affairs. With the Bible, Cranmer enclosed a letter dated 4 August 1537 from Ford, warmly commending the new translation: 'As for the translation, so far as I have read thereof, I like it better than any other translation heretofore made; yet not doubting but that there may, and will be found some faults therein, as you know no man ever did, or can do so well, but it may be from time to time amended.'

He spoke of the great care and labour in its preparation and praised particularly the dedication to the king, to whom he begged the minister to present it and to obtain, if possible, the royal license 'that the same may be sold and read by every person, without danger of any Act, proclamation or ordinance granted up to now to the contrary, until such time that we, the bishops, shall set forth a better translation, which I think will not be till a day after doomsday' [a reference to a failed attempt to get the Bible translated into English by 'good and learned men' back in 1534].

He also warned that those who favoured the book would suffer 'some snubs, many slanders, lies and reproaches' because of the supposed heretical notes. The main objection, though, would be because it was a Bible in English for everyone to read.

A second letter from Cranmer to Cromwell

Cromwell acted on this advice immediately, which suggests that he had already made his own plans for the Bible and that he caught the king in a particularly generous mood. After Henry had licensed it for distribution Grafton sent six copies to Cromwell as a gift. But Cromwell insisted on paying for the copies, sending £10 to Grafton, with a note saying that no favour was required on account of the licence.

Thomas Cromwell, earl of Essex

Only nine days after the first letter, on 13 August, Cranmer wrote to him again, thanking him warmly for having effected the object he desired and assuring him that his having obtained the king's licence for the introduction of this Bible gave him more pleasure than a gift of a thousand pounds. 'I doubt not,' continued Cranmer, 'but that hereby such fruit of good knowledge shall follow that it shall well appear hereafter what high and acceptable good you have done to God and the king, which shall so much redound to your honour that, besides God's reward, you shall obtain perpetual memory for the same within this realm. And as for me, you may reckon me your bondman for the same. And I dare be bold to say, so may you do my Lord of Worcester [Hugh Latimer].' Latimer showed his gratitude for the translation by immediately repeating the 1536 vicegerent's order for Bibles in his own diocesan injunctions that autumn, and other bishops followed his lead.

A third letter from Cranmer to Cromwell

On 28 August, Cranmer again wrote to Cromwell: 'This shall be to give you most hearty thanks that any heart can think, and that in the name of them all who favour God's word, for your diligence at this time in procuring the king's highness to set forth the said God's word and his gospel by his grace's authority; for the which act not only the king's majesty, but also you shall have perpetual praise and memory of all them that be now and hereafter shall be God's faithful people and the favourers of his word.' Without doubt Cranmer recognized the superiority of the translation and rejoiced at its publication.

The acceptance of the Matthew's Bible

In many ways it is remarkable that the Matthew's Bible was so quickly received. Initially it had no powerful friend to proclaim its merits or urge its claims, and was only protected by a poor printer who had invested his all in its success; and yet it was immediately accepted with great joy by the archbishop of Canterbury, the highest religious dignitary in the land, who at once commended it to Lord Cromwell, who in turn presented it to the king himself. The king, without the slightest hesitation, gave it the royal endorsement. Surely God was bringing glory to his name by working out his purpose through some of the most powerful men, religiously and politically, of the time.

Letters from Grafton to Cromwell

On the same day as Cranmer's third letter, 28 August 1537, Richard Grafton wrote to Cromwell. With one eye on the results of his pecuniary investment, and the other on the excitement that ruled the hour, he asked Cromwell, in the most flattering terms, if he would add to the royal licence already publicly announced the formality of his official seal, which was equivalent to today's copyright. What he was after was a monopoly of the publication of the Bible.

Cromwell declined the request and so Grafton wrote to him again, highlighting the fact that he had invested his whole fortune of £500 in the undertaking and already issued 1500 copies (a large number for those days) of the work. He claimed that as the work had been received so well in high quarters and a demand created for it, that others, less conscientious than himself, would print cheaper and imperfect editions, thus interfering with the profit that should be his alone. His real motive for desiring the official seal was because it would be his 'making and wealth'. He had no thought for the word of God, only for his own selfish desires. He pleaded with Cromwell to prevent the 'undoing of a poor young man'.

He then suggested that Cromwell could compel the curate of every parish to buy a copy for the use of his charge, and every abbey to buy six copies to be placed in many different places for the convenience of the people. Once again he unveiled his selfish motives when he said that 'none other but they of the Catholicical sort should be compelled to have them'.

He assured Cromwell that his cooperation would be 'a godly act, worthy to be had in remembrance while the world does stand'.

Royal injunctions

In many ways Grafton was expressing a growing consensus that, as a matter of principle, the people of England should be allowed to hear and read the Bible in their own language, although others worked from the belief that the most effective way of countering the influence of potentially seditious unauthorized translations was to flood the country with reliable and safe translations, and insist that these be read out loud during regular public worship.

Cromwell not only encouraged bishops to order copies for their churches, but he managed to obtain a royal proclamation that a copy of this Bible should be provided by every parish church for the open and free use of the people. It was published in the name of the king on 3 September 1538, and charged the clergy of the church to 'provide, on this side of the feast of All Saints next coming, one book of the whole Bible of the largest volume in English, and the same set up in some convenient place within the said church that you have cure of, whereas your parishioners may most commodiously resort to the same and read it. The charges of which book shall be rateably borne between you, the parson and the parishioners aforesaid, that is to say, the one half by you and the other half by them.'

The king may have authorized the use of such a Bible, but he certainly was not going to pay for it, preferring to leave it as the product of private enterprise and entrepreneurship. The reference to 'the largest volume in English' is undoubtedly a reference to the size of the Matthew's Bible, which was ideally suited for church use. Coverdale's 1535 version (27·8cm by 18·6cm) was too small to be used on most church lecterns.

The parishioners were urged to read the Bible, 'the very lively word of God, that

Miles Coverdale

every Christian is bound to embrace, believe and follow, if he look to be saved'. The clergy were exhorted to 'declare the very gospel of Christ', and the people were warned not to 'repose their trust in other works devised by men's fantasies besides Scripture, as in wandering to pilgrimages, offering of money, candles or tapers to feigned relics or images, or kissing or licking the same, saying over a number of beads not understood nor minded on, or such like superstitions, for the doing whereof you not only have no promise of reward in Scripture, but contrariwise great threats and maledictions of God, as things tending to idolatry and superstitions, which of all offences, God always does most detest and abhor, for that the same diminishes most his honour and glory'.

The only restriction concerning the use of the Bible was that all who read it should not discuss its merits in public places. Further, any constructions of its doctrines were to be kept quiet. All doubts and difficulties were to be determined by the regularly appointed preachers and teachers.

In this proclamation the king assented to the sentence that all things contained in this book expressed 'the undoubted will, law and commandment of Almighty God', a statement that he was soon to ignore.

Cromwell's support and death
Cromwell found that there were simply not enough copies available, especially as he wanted to place one in every parish church in the land, of which there were nearly 9,000. Reprinting the Matthew's Bible on a large scale would create hostility from those who recognized the initials WT in that work, so he decided, with Cranmer's encouragement, to employ Coverdale to revise the Matthew's Bible. Changes would be kept to a minimum and most of the marginal notes removed to make it more acceptable to conservative bishops who were suspicious of Reformers' annotations. It was going to be a large folio (33·7cm by 23·5cm) placed in every church, prominent and easy to read either alone or to a congregation. Grafton and Whitchurch were to publish it and it was to be printed in Paris. It became known, probably because of its size, as 'the Great Bible'.

It is worth mentioning at this point that Thomas Cromwell, afterwards earl of Essex, was then at the zenith of his power, occupying an eminence next only to that of the king himself. His religious policies demonstrate sympathy for Lutheran doctrines, although he went to his death protesting his loyalty and orthodoxy. Inevitably his Protestant leanings stirred up opposition and his attempt to establish an alliance with Lutheran princes by way of marriage did not last long—the more so because Anne of Cleves was so unattractive to Henry. His subsequent disgrace and downfall were unmerited and no serious charge was ever sustained. By no means perfect, he was, according to some, the best minister Henry VIII ever had. He was beheaded at Tower Hill on 28 July 1540, having been hurriedly condemned without a trial for heresy and treason (he was guilty of neither) under the Act of Attainder.

Rogers was not chosen to prepare 'the Great Bible'

Grafton managed to dispose of his 1,500 copies of the Matthew's Bible. A year later he was in Paris, engaged with Coverdale in making preparations for 'the Great Bible'.

'The Great Bible' (courtesy of www.greatsite.com)

It seems that Rogers was not chosen for this important work for the following reasons: Cromwell had the power to employ whoever he wanted and Coverdale was his old favourite; although Coverdale lacked Hebrew and Greek, he was a good Latinist and able to tweak the Bible, especially the non-Tyndale half of the Old Testament, back towards the 'Latin original', which would satisfy those critics who regarded Hebrew and Greek as 'subversive interlopers'; Rogers was a busy pastor and would not be tempted to leave his charge for a work that could be accomplished by an ordinary scholar; he also knew from his former experience that Grafton would not follow his counsel or judgement in the second edition any more than he had followed them in the first edition. Another reason is that he could not safely return to England to consult with the interested parties as, by that time, he was a married priest and as such he would be an offence to the church and state.

Rogers probably had no further connection with the Matthew's Bible, although he may have superintended some of the editions afterwards published by John Day and others. As has been said, Coverdale made few serious alterations to the text of the Matthew's Bible. Some of the prefaces and prologues were withdrawn as well as the marginal notes that had been introduced by Rogers, but the integrity of the volume was not affected.

The *Interim*

Although there is little news of Rogers's activities at this time, until after the death of Henry VIII, the battle between the Reformers and traditionalists continued to rage. 'The Great Bible' became the only English Bible authorized for public use (the 'Authorized Version' of 1611 was never actually authorized) and was distributed to every church and chained to the pulpit. Several editions were printed between 1539 and 1541 and printers and sellers of books were encouraged to provide for the 'free and liberal use of the Bible in our own maternal English tongue'. By the decree of the king every church was to provide a reader so that the illiterate could hear and understand God's word. According to contemporary evidence, 'the Great Bible' was welcomed and read with avidity.

Act of the Six Articles

In the same year as 'the Great Bible' was printed, the first official undoing of reform was passed: the Act of the Six Articles, which modified and consolidated existing laws against heresy and reasserted traditional Catholic doctrine as the basis of faith for the English Church. It became known as the 'whip with six strings' for its severity and was a weighty counter-move back to Rome. Anyone found teaching, practising or even believing anything contrary to the Articles was liable to severe punishment, including fines, forfeiture of property, imprisonment and execution. Archbishops and bishops were to hold periodic commissions of inquiry in every county of England and Wales to examine and pass sentence on offenders, and the commissioners were empowered to seize and destroy all books that contained anything against the Articles.

The first article asserted the Catholic principle of transubstantiation at mass; anyone refusing this doctrine would be burnt as a heretic. Refusal to adopt the other five Articles—communion under one kind only, the legality of clerical celibacy, the sanctity of monastic vows, the justness of private masses and the need for aural confession—was punishable by hanging. Under these draconian new powers, a vigorous campaign against heresy was launched in London in the king's name.

Henry thus demonstrated that he was prepared to enforce under heavy penalties the fundamental doctrines of the Catholic Church. Approved by Convocation and enacted by Parliament in June, the statute arose from the king's personal conservatism in matters of doctrine, from his need for better relations with the Catholic powers of Spain and France, and from his desire to curb the growth of 'heresy' in England and religious unrest in Calais. In protest Latimer resigned his See, while Cranmer was forced to send his wife back to Germany. Others fled abroad or were imprisoned.

The Bible under attack

The king's proclamation to set up the Bible in every church was followed by a command that any uncertainty about the meaning of Scripture should be interpreted by 'such learned men as be or shall be authorized to preach and declare the same', the aim of which was 'discreet quietness and sober moderation', which was a coded way of demanding 'unquestioning obedience'. In 1543 Parliament passed an Act 'for the advancement of true religion and for the abolishment of the contrary', which banned Tyndale's translation. It became a crime for any unlicensed person to read or expound the Bible publicly to others, and the lower classes were not even allowed to read the Bible privately. Three years later Henry issued a proclamation forbidding all men and women 'to receive, have, take, or keep, Tyndale's or Coverdale's New Testament'. In London large quantities of the forbidden books were collected and burned at St Paul's Cross under the initiative of the Bishop of London, Edmund Bonner.

Henry's death, Edward's accession

Henry VIII died in January 1547, with Cranmer by his side. The archbishop, 'exhorting him to put his trust in Christ and to call on his mercy, desired him, though he could not speak, yet to give some token with his eyes or with his hand, that he trusted in the Lord. Then the king, holding him with his hand, did wring his hand in his as hard as he could.'

Edward VI's accession to the throne of England on 28 January 1547 heralded a new era in the history of the country and especially of the church. His enthronement was accompanied by the appointment of a 'protector', Edward Seymour, the king's uncle, who was given the new title

Edward VI, the boy-king

duke of Somerset. He and his supporters were favourable to reform, and they brought about 'sweeping changes in the religious life of the nation'. Those who had been imprisoned under the Act of the Six Articles were released, including Latimer, who had spent a year in the Tower of London.

These appointments were also welcome signs to many Christians who had left the country from religious motives during the latter part of Henry's reign to return. Some hurried home immediately, while others waited to see the character of the government surrounding the boy-king. Rogers did not return straightaway, probably because he did not want to sever suddenly his connection with his German congregation or to leave his good friends Melanchthon and others to whom he had become attached. Speaking of Rogers's integrity, trustworthiness and constancy, Melanchthon called his comrade a 'learned man ... gifted with great ability which he sets off with a noble character'.

The *Interim of Augsburg*

Rogers appears next through his involvement with the *Augsburg Interim*, which was a temporary doctrinal agreement between German Catholics and Protestants, proclaimed in May 1548 at the Diet of Augsburg (1547–48), which became imperial law in June 1548. It was prepared and accepted at the insistence of the Holy Roman emperor Charles V, who hoped to establish temporary religious unity in Germany until differences could be worked out in a general Council of the Catholic Church.

The *Interim* consisted of twenty-six articles concerning matters of doctrine and ecclesiastical discipline. The points of doctrine were all explained in the sense of Catholic dogma, but couched in mild and vague terms; and wherever it was feasible, the form and the concept approached the Protestant view on those subjects. In matters of ecclesiastical discipline two important concessions were made to the Protestants concerning the marriage of priests and communion in both kinds (bread and wine) for the laity. The *Interim* declared that all Charles's Catholic dominions should inviolably observe the customs, statutes and ordinances of the universal church, and that those who were separate from it, should either reunite themselves to it or at least conform themselves to its constitution.

Rejected

However, the *Interim* pleased neither the Pope nor the Protestants. The Pope designed to send some prelates to the emperor to correct it, but Cardinal Moore and some bishops advised him against it, saying it was but a bare toleration of a small part of Lutheranism, with a great restriction against the rest. The Lutheran preachers said they would not receive it. Martin Bucer, minister of Strasburg, refused to sign it, alleging that it re-established Popery; other ministers of the chief Protestant cities chose rather to quit their chairs and livings and withdraw to Prussia and Switzerland, than subscribe to it; the duke of Germany rejected it; Calvin and several others wrote against it; and Robert Cenalis, bishop of Avranches, refuted it in his book *The Antidote*. In the words of Rogers, the *Interim* commanded that all the cities in Germany that had received the word of God and made a change of ceremonies accordingly, should reform their churches again and turn to the old Popish ordinances, 'as a dog does to that he has spewed out, or a washed swine to the mire'.

Charles V was so angry with those who refused it that he disfranchised the cities of Magdeburg and Constance for their opposition. His attempts to force it through led the Protestants to adopt the *Leipzig Interim*, which upheld Protestant doctrines, at the Diet of Leipzig in December 1548. Neither interim was fully accepted and a German religious settlement was not brought about until the Peace of Augsburg in 1555, the year Rogers was martyred.

Weighing and Considering of the Interim

The exact time of Rogers's return to England is not known; however, he was in London by 1 August 1548 for he dated the preface to his translation of Melanchthon's *Weighing and Considering of the Interim* on that day and added 'at London, in Edward Whitchurch's house', where he was evidently living at that time. Some think he was simply visiting England in order to see if it was practicable and safe to move his wife and eight children, for we hear nothing of him again until May 1550, but this is unlikely.

Melanchthon's small tract plainly answered the greatest misuses of the Roman bishop's 'most tyrannous kingdom'. He showed to what things a

Christian may agree, which things may be changed and which not. It was sent to England, printed in English and was on sale in London within two months of the time that the emperor's edict was first issued, quite a feat for the sixteenth century. At the time of its publication it was an important work and is often referred to in contemporaneous literature.

Rogers's translation of *Weighing and Considering of the Interim* was not only a tribute to his friend, whose society in Germany he had only recently left, but it also served to quash the rumours that the German reformer had abandoned the Protestant faith and returned to Popery. In the first paragraph of the preface Rogers demonstrates that constancy and firmness which he was to show during his own persecutions. He also mentions that he had received a letter from a godly and scholarly man, who said that 'learned men' in Germany were ready to refute and stand against the *Interim*.

By translating the work Rogers wanted to comfort 'many godly and Christian hearts, who have been not a little dismayed and discouraged through such lies [of Melanchthon's defection]. And verily not without cause, for his denying would do more harm to the truth in these last and most perilous times, than any tongue or pen can express... At this time also, thanks be to God therefore, he has not only not denied the truth, but also after his old accustomed Christian manner, plainly confessed and acknowledged it, which thing this his answer to the *Interim*, enough witnesses.'

Joan of Kent

It is important at this stage to mention an incident in the history of Rogers, the original of which is found only in the Latin edition (1559) of John Foxe. It concerns the Anabaptist martyr Joan Bocher (also Boucher or Butcher), commonly known as Joan of Kent and Joan Knel, who was condemned to death by evangelical bishops for heresy. She first came to notice about 1540 as 'a great dispenser of Tyndale's New Testament', which she carried under her clothing to the ladies of Henry VIII's court. She was a 'great reader of Scripture' and a good friend of Anne Askew, who was burnt for heresy in 1546. She also visited prisoners and used her wealth to relieve those suffering for their faith.

Before 1543 she had adopted opinions about the incarnation of Christ that were at odds with both Protestant and Catholic orthodoxy, and she was charged with heresy, but Henry VIII had interfered to stop proceedings against her at that time.

She was in trouble again in 1548, during Edward VI's reign, when she was arrested and imprisoned for her unusual views. The record of the 'bewildering charge' against her in the archbishop's register reads: 'That you believe that the Word was made flesh in the virgin's belly; but that Christ took flesh of the virgin, you believe not, because the flesh of the virgin, being the outward man, was sinfully gotten and born in sin: but the Word, by the consent of the inward man of the virgin, was made flesh.' It seems she held an eccentric and erroneous belief that Mary had two seeds, one natural and one spiritual, and that Christ was the spiritual seed. It must be said, however, that she believed Mary was a virgin when Jesus was born and that she accepted Christ as the virgin-born Son of God.

In our present day it is extraordinary how the leaders of the church at that time could magnify doctrinal error into a crime deserving death, but these men had high principles and were contending for great ends and, on that basis, anyone who opposed the truth as they understood it had to be removed. The spread of such sentiments, they argued, even to a limited degree, might threaten the cause for which they were working so hard to establish. In the case of Joan of Kent, who had evidently been prominent in propagating a heresy, an example had to be made.

Condemned

In 1547 the government had secured the parliamentary repeal of all previous heresy legislation which had permitted the burning of heretics, so in the setting up of the heresy tribunals against radicals in 1548 and 1549, it had to rely on the residual common-law powers of the Crown over heresy to get its way, and in so doing it reached the same end as the old heresy laws.

In 1549, on the very same day that a royal commission against heresy was issued, Joan of Kent, 'the formidable veteran radical whose christological views seem to have developed dramatically away from orthodoxy in the opening years of Edward's reign', was examined under the chairmanship of Archbishop Thomas Cranmer, and during her trial she insisted that Christ did not 'take flesh of the virgin'. According to Latimer, one of the members of the commission, she said that 'our Saviour had a phantastical body'. As a result Cranmer, who read out the charge in the Lady Chapel of St Paul's Cathedral on 12 April 1549, judicially excommunicated her. Latimer later said, 'She would say that our Saviour was not very man, nor had received flesh of his mother Mary, and yet she could show no reason why she believed so. Her opinion was this: the Son of God penetrated through her as through a glass, taking no substance of her.' From this statement it appears she was condemned, not simply because of her peculiar opinions, but because she could not support them by reasoned arguments.

At the end of April, Cranmer sent a detailed account of her heresy and of his proceedings against her to Edward VI and handed her over to the Privy Council for punishment. She was sent back to prison for a year 'while the government dithered about how to handle such an embarrassingly awkward would-be martyr'. During that time various Protestant clergymen visited her, but they failed to induce her to change her mind. For a while she was detained by Lord Chancellor Rich in his own residence, where Cranmer and Ridley visited her almost daily; 'but she was so high in spirit that they could do nothing with her'.

On 27 April 1550 Lord Chancellor Rich, in accordance with an order of the Council, issued a writ to the sheriff of London to burn her, and 2 May was the appointed day for her execution in Smithfield. Her crime: 'certain detestable opinions of heresy'. Dr Scory, afterwards bishop of Rochester, 'preached at her death' and was reviled by Joan as a lying rogue. From all accounts she suffered bravely and when the sentence of condemnation was announced, she said to the tribunal, 'It is a godly matter to consider your ignorance. It was not long ago since you burned Anne Askew for a piece of bread, and yet came yourselves soon after to believe and profess the same doctrine for which you burned her. And now, forsooth, you will needs to burn me for a piece of flesh [the Lord's body], and in the end you will come to believe this also, when you have read the Scriptures and understood them.'

Burnet rightly condemns the policy that led the Protestant Reformers to burn Joan, a supporter of their own party, adding, 'The woman's carriage made her be looked on as a frantic person fitter for Bedlam than a stake.' Certainly her death has left a black mark against the conduct of the Reformers.

An appeal made to John Rogers

As has been said Joan of Kent was condemned on 27 April 1550 and executed on 2 May. During the intervening five days an interesting conversation took place. A friend (possibly Foxe himself, who deplored all executions for religion, even of those who were clearly in error) went to Rogers, and exhorted and beseeched him to use his influence with the archbishop of Canterbury, pleading that as her error had been as far as possible punished and restrained by imprisonment, her life should be spared. He argued that in time her fault might be cured; that if she lived, she would only corrupt a few persons; but if she suffered death for her opinions, others might be tempted by her courage to adopt them. He urged that she might remain in prison where she could not influence weak minds and be allowed every opportunity to repent.

This earnest petition, however, made no impression on Rogers, who stuck to his opinion that she should suffer death by burning. His friend renewed his appeal, saying that if she was to die, some other mode of death

The burning of Anne Askew

might be selected, more in accordance with the gentleness and mercy taught in the gospel. He protested against the introduction into the Christian code of justice, in imitation of the Catholics, the horrors of such a tormenting death. In response Rogers declared that death by burning was the least agonizing of all and sufficiently 'gentle'.

His friend, who thought Rogers had little concern for the unfortunate woman, in great passion, hit Rogers's hand, which he had been holding tightly, and said prophetically, 'Well then, maybe you will find out that on some occasion you yourself will have your hands full of this same gentle burning.' Of course, Rogers, in just a few years time, was the first martyr to suffer by burning in the reign of Mary I.

It is hardly surprising that those opposed to the Protestant Church condemned for many years such an execution, even well into Elizabeth's reign, and some regarded the deaths of Cranmer and Ridley as a divine vengeance for the burning of Joan of Kent. Later William Cobbett, whose *History of the Protestant Reformation* (1829) was frequently reprinted by Roman Catholic presses, said of Cranmer that his name could not be pronounced 'without almost doubting of the justice of God, were it not for our knowledge of the fact, that the cold-blooded, most perfidious man expired at last amidst those flames which he himself had been the chief cause of kindling'. Even John Foxe, a great supporter of Cranmer, spread an unlikely tale that the archbishop 'bullied a reluctant Edward VI into signing Joan's death warrant'.

Perhaps we could be equally scathing about Rogers, who turned down the chance to speak in her defence and to save her from the stake. Roger Hutchinson in his *Image of God* claimed it was Rogers's responsibility to excommunicate Anabaptist offenders, hand them over to the civil magistrate and then let the law take its course, whether that meant death or not for the 'heretic'. Rogers's view and subsequent behaviour, however deplorable in the twenty-first century, was not uncommon among Tudor evangelicals. Archdeacon John Philpot, for instance, when confronted with his own death by burning in Mary's reign, still maintained that Joan of Kent was 'well worthy to be burnt'.

Appointments and Ridley's support

Rogers loved England and always worked for its good, although he was only too aware of the dangers to the gospel that lurked in the corridors of power. 'I am an Englishman born, and God knows, do naturally wish well to my country. I have often proved that the things which I have feared aforehand have indeed followed. I pray God that I may fail of my guessing in this behalf; but truly, that will not be with expelling the true word of God out of the realm and with the shedding of innocent blood.'

In the Latin edition of Foxe, the author says more strongly that Rogers, 'thinking it the duty of every good man to devote his best abilities to his own country—although, where he was preaching, his position and prospects were highly honourable and even lucrative—preferred to abandon his worldly fortune, rather than disregard the calls of that duty. Having returned, therefore, to his native land he manfully devoted himself to furthering the work of the gospel, labouring willingly and earnestly; and it was not long before his labours were personally rewarded' by the presentations mentioned below.

St Margaret and St Sepulchre

On 10 May 1550, a week or so after Joan of Kent's execution, Rogers was presented simultaneously to the rectory of St Margaret Moyses and the vicarage of St Sepulchre, both in London. In both cases the patronage was directly in the Crown, but the presentation to St Sepulchre was made by 'Nicof. Yertswort, *pro hac vice*'—probably identical with Nicasius Yetswiert, whose daughter became the wife of Daniel Rogers, one of the sons of the martyr. He succeeded to St Margaret Moyses on the death of Robert Johnson and to St Sepulchre on that of William Copeland.

St Margaret then stood on the east side of Friday Street, over against Distaff Lane end, and was sometimes called St Margaret in Friday Street. Rogers was the thirty-eighth rector in succession. The great fire destroyed the building, after which the parish was annexed to St Mildred, and the church of that name in Bread Street came to represent both parishes.

St Sepulchre without Newgate

Rogers was the eighth vicar in succession at St Sepulchre and this important position, which included a parsonage house, was one of the most lucrative in the gift of the Crown. The fire of 1666 also destroyed this church, except for the walls and tower. Ironically, the porch of St Sepulchre overlooked Newgate jail, notorious for its inhumane treatment of prisoners and the place where Rogers was later confined. St Sepulchre was often a stop where prisoners sentenced to the gallows at Tyburn, which was first established in 1571, would be 'treated' to a final drink. The *Newgate Chronicler* reports that a tradition was established at St Sepulchre of tolling the funeral bell (still in the church in a glass case) to arouse Newgate prisoners on their final night, with the accompanying cry, 'All you who in the condemned hole do lie, prepare you, for tomorrow you shall die.' At one time the prisoners were hanged on a gallows in the street outside the prison, and many of the spectators must have raised their eyes to the tower of St Sepulchre as they watched the prisoners swinging lifelessly from the ropes.

Newgate's execution bell

These appointments are worthy of note because they

indicate the estimation in which Rogers was held in the highest quarters. So valuable a vicarage as well as a rectory, and shortly afterwards a prebendal stall in the cathedral church, would not have been given to just anyone, especially to one who had returned to England a comparative stranger to those who might have helped him by their wealth and influence. These presentations must have been made to him on account of his personal character and abilities.

St Pancras and St Paul's

Rogers was appointed prebendal stall of St Pancras, then vacant by the death of John Royston, on 24 August 1551, by which time he had been occupied with the work of his two parishes for some fifteen months and had been in England for more than three years.

The prebend of St Pancras appears to have been one of the most valuable in the list as far as revenues were concerned and was presented to him by his old acquaintance Nicholas Ridley, then bishop of London, who, along with Rogers, had been educated at Pembroke Hall, Cambridge. Ridley must have been aware of Rogers's work and ministrations at Wittenberg and Meldorf and the great abilities he showed after his return to London, which probably influenced his decision.

The rectory of Chigwell in Essex was attached to the prebend, but the previous incumbent had in 1540 leased the living for thirty-one years on such terms that Rogers could derive no pecuniary benefit from it during the time of the lease. However, the title rector of Chigwell must be added to the list of Rogers's titles.

Rogers preached for a time with great success, which moved Ridley to give him a prebend in the cathedral church of St Paul's. However, all this extra responsibility proved too much for Rogers, for on 10 September 1551, he resigned the rectorship of St Margaret Moyses.

Ridley's first letter

Ridley held Rogers, along with his two fellow labourers in the gospel, Edmund Grindal and John Bradford, in high esteem and regarded their work as indispensable to the success of the Reformation. Two extracts from Ridley's letters are enough to show the regard in which he held these men. The first was written to Sir John Cheke, an English classical scholar and statesman and a strong supporter of the Protestant Reformation, on 23 July 1551.

Nicholas Ridley

I have gotten the good will, and grant to be with me, of three preachers, men of good learning, and, as I am persuaded, of excellent virtue; which are able, both with life and learning, to set forth God's Word in London, and in the whole diocese of the same, where is most need of all parts in England. For from thence goes example, as you know, into all the rest of the King's Majesty's whole realm. The men's names be these: Master Grindal, whom you know to be a man of virtue and learning; Master Bradford, a man by whom (as I am assuredly informed) God has and does work wonders in setting forth of his Word; the third [John Rogers?] is a preacher, the which, for detecting and confuting of the Anabaptists and Catholics [in Essex], both by his preaching and by his writing, is enforced now to bear Christ's cross. The two first be scholars in the University: the third is as poor as either of the other two.

Ridley seems to suggest that Rogers was already experiencing persecution, but it probably means that he was already opposed by the Catholics and other enemies of the Reformation, against whom he had been preaching and writing. Men such as Gardiner and Bonner were bitterly opposed to all he said and did and heaped on him the severest slanders in retaliation for what he said against their creed. It is likely that Rogers published certain works at this time in support of Protestantism and against its enemies, but no record can be found to prove that point. Maybe he was a sort of champion, who made the most of every opportunity to dispute with the adversaries of the new faith from the pulpit and through the press. He was certainly occupied with preaching outside his special charges in London.

The reference to poverty is harder to resolve, for certainly the revenues from the various offices which he had held for some time would have produced a considerable sum and one quite adequate to support his large family. Perhaps Ridley was not referring to Rogers at all. He certainly seems to imply that the third man was not a scholar in the university; and yet Ridley and Rogers had been fellow-students in the same college at Cambridge. It may be that Ridley was speaking of Edmund West, one of his chaplains and the third one of his candidates for the vacant prebends. Sadly, West recanted early in Mary's reign and even tried to persuade Ridley to do the same. He seems to have been so affected by his own weakness and disgrace that he died from the effects of excessive grief about May 1554.

Ridley's second letter

The second letter was written on 18 November 1552 to Sir John Gates, vice-chamberlain and captain of the guard, and Sir William Cecil, Chancellor of the Order of the Garter: 'Now, good Mr Vice-Chamberlain and Mr Secretary, you know both how I did bestow of late three or four prebends which did fall in my time, and what manner of men they be to whom I gave them, Grindal, Bradford, and Rogers, men known to be so necessary to be abroad in the commonwealth, that I can keep none of them with me in my house.'

The following endorsement was written on the back of this letter, probably by one of the persons to whom it was addressed: 'November 1552—The bishop of London to Sir John Gates and Sir William Cecil—Learned preachers: Bradford, Rogers, Grindal, Grimald, Sampson, Harvey, Ridley. To succeed in the chauntership of Paul's, to be void by Grindal's going to be bishop in the north.' Lines were subsequently drawn across this entry, probably when it was determined not to make the change contemplated.

Edmund Grindal

When Ridley became bishop of London, he made Grindal one of his chaplains and gave him the precentorship of St Paul's Cathedral. He was soon promoted to be one of Edward's chaplains and prebendary of Westminster, and in October 1552 was one of six to whom the forty-two articles were submitted for examination before being sanctioned by the

Privy Council. According to John Knox, Grindal distinguished himself from most of the court preachers in 1553 by denouncing the worldliness of courtiers and foretelling the evils that would follow the king's death. For this reason, Grindal was not made a bishop and did not consider himself bound to await the evils he had foretold. On the accession of Queen Mary he fled to Strasbourg. He returned to England in 1559 and became successively bishop of London, archbishop of York and finally archbishop of Canterbury. After Grindal's escape, Bradford and Rogers were left without his support to face the fiery trial of persecution.

Edmund Grindal of St Bees

John Bradford

In 1550 Bradford was ordained by Ridley and shortly afterwards appointed by Edward VI to be one of the six royal chaplains who were sent about England, with a kind of roving commission, to preach up the doctrines of the Reformation. However, within a month of Mary's accession he was arrested on a charge of 'preaching seditious sermons' and confined to the Tower, where he wrote his treatise *The Hurt of Hearing Mass*. For a time he was lodged in the same single cell as Cranmer, Ridley and Latimer, the Tower being then full owing to the imprisonment of Sir Thomas Wyatt and his supporters, who had violently opposed Mary's proposed Spanish marriage. Their time together was spent reading the New Testament 'with great deliberation and painful study'. Bradford was transferred to the King's Bench prison and then to the Compter in the Poultry. He was condemned as an 'obstinate heretic'.

On 30 June 1555, nearly five months after Rogers's death, Bradford was taken to Newgate and the following day burned at the stake. A great crowd, made up of many who admired Bradford, came to witness the execution. As he stood by the stake he held up his hands, looked to heaven and cried out, 'O England, England, repent you of your sins, repent you of your sins. Beware of idolatry, beware of false antichrists; take heed they do not deceive you.' He then turned to fellow-martyr, John Leaf, and said, 'Be of good comfort, brother; for we shall have a merry supper with the Lord this night!' His last words were: 'Strait is the way and narrow is the gate that leads to salvation, and few there be that find it.' A writer of his period recorded that he endured the flames 'as a fresh gale of wind in a hot summer's day, confirming by his death the truth of that doctrine he had so diligently and powerfully preached during his life'.

John Bradford

Divinity Lecturer in St Paul's

It is uncertain when exactly Rogers was chosen by the dean and chapter to the office of Divinity Lecturer in St Paul's. In both the Latin and English editions of Foxe, it appears to be suggested that it was nearly simultaneous with his appointment to the prebend (August 1551); but in a list of the acts assented to by Edward VI and his Privy Council, there is one dated June 1553, being 'a presentation to the bishop of London, to admit John Rogers within the cathedral church of Saint Paul, in London'. If this refers to the same event, then Rogers had held his prebend for nearly two years before he was chosen to the lectureship, the duties of which he only performed for a very short time, for not long afterwards he was confined as a prisoner in his own house.

Perhaps the only way to reconcile this discrepancy is to say that Rogers had been previously chosen to the office and had been for some time fulfilling its requirements, but that the official recognition of the king and Council had been, for some reason, delayed until that later date.

The countdown to persecution

Rogers was not a man to remain silent when he saw abuses taking place either in the church or in the civil government, but condemned them in that bold and uncompromising manner that he afterwards displayed in his examinations just before his death. For instance, he preached boldly and powerfully against the misuse of abbey lands by Northumberland and his party. This forceful approach led him into difficulties with the authorities even during Edward's reign.

Controversy about priests' garments

Rogers at this time was not so much opposed to the general tenets of the church but to some minor outward customs, which he thought savoured too much of Popery. One of the customs he disliked was the custom of the regular clergy, when they went out, to wear their priests' coats and square caps and in some cases gowns and tippets. Quite a controversy arose among the bishops and clergy, and some of the preachers refused to wear these distinctive garments, even though convocation and parliament had prescribed them.

Rogers was at the forefront of this debate and, in this respect, he defied the authority of the church and the government, living in open disobedience to both and satisfying himself that the requirements were against his conscience. He was appealed to and reasoned with on the subject, but refused ever to wear anything other than a round cap. He affirmed that he would not agree to a decree of uniformity, but on this condition, that if they needed to have such a uniformity of wearing the cap, tippet, etc., then it should also be decreed that the Catholics, to make a difference between them and others, should be forced to wear on their sleeves a chalice with a host on it. If they would consent to that, he would agree to wear the priestly garments. He knew very well that this proposition would never be accepted.

This seems to have put an end to the controversy as far as he was concerned. He continued to wear the round cap as long as he lived and was never again criticized for doing so.

Naturalization of his wife and children

In 1552 Rogers proved his loyalty and patriotism by securing, through a special act of parliament, the legal naturalization of his wife and those of his children who were born in Germany. In the latter part of March, in connection with other preachers, he presented a petition, which stated, that while pursuing their studies beyond the sea, they had married certain women born in those parts by whom they had had children, who intended, by God's grace, to become his Majesty's faithful and obedient subjects. They requested that both their wives and children might be 'reputed and taken as the king's natural subjects as lawful persons born within this realm of England'.

The petition was read for the first time in the House of Lords on 31 March; it was finally passed by the Commons on 9 April, but not without some opposition, and received the royal assent on 15 of the same month. The original act bears the autograph of Edward VI in his schoolboy handwriting.

Edward VI's death

The real troubles for Rogers and the Reformation began when Edward VI died on 6 July 1553. Rogers appreciated the work that the boy-king had done to advance Protestantism, writing, 'King Edward also, by parliament, according to God's word, set the marriage of priests at liberty, abolished the Popish and idolatrous mass, changed the Latin service, and set up the holy communion; the whole clergy consented hereto, many of them set it forth by their preaching; and all they by practising confirmed the same.' However, such reforms and the men who upheld them were about to be severely tested—a testing that was inaugurated by the events that took place at St Paul's Cross.

St Paul's Cross

St Paul's Preaching Cross, in St Paul's Cathedral churchyard, was the setting, and perhaps to some extent the inspiration, of some of the most interesting scenes in the story of London. Certainly, if a complete set of the sermons delivered at the Cross were collected, there would be quite a detailed history of the Anglican Church. The Cross was rebuilt by Thomas Kemp in the late fifteenth century, with such imposing grandeur and grace of form that it became one of the outstanding decorative features of London. It was an open-air pulpit, largely made of timber and mounted on steps of stone, with a lead-roof and a low wall around. There was room in it for three or four persons.

Before it became the pulpit of the cathedral, it was the traditional site for the announcement of general proclamations, civil as well as religious in nature, and the place where Londoners gathered in the management of their own affairs or in times of national crisis. Papal bulls, excommunications, public confessions and recantations of heresy were all made known at the Cross; impostors and frauds were exposed there; and royal edicts, public proclamations, national addresses, denunciation of traitors, victories by sea and land, royal marriages and deaths were all publicized at that spot. It has been said that 'all the Reformation was accomplished from the Cross'.

Ridley's sermon

On Sunday 9 July 1553, three days after Edward's death and on the very day that Mary had herself proclaimed queen, Nicholas Ridley, by order of the Council, preached a sermon at Paul's Cross, in which he denounced in the strongest terms the princess Mary, whom he represented as a thorough Catholic, who would, if she succeeded to the throne, restore the Papal dominion and betray the kingdom to a foreign power. He also contrasted her character and her probable government with that of Lady Jane Grey, who was to be proclaimed queen the next day, and declared both Mary and Elizabeth to be illegitimate. It is not surprising that Mary remembered this vitriol when she came to power and it virtually sealed Ridley's doom from the moment it was delivered.

Rogers's first sermon

On the following Sunday, 16 July, when the battle between Lady Jane's

Lady Jane Grey

and Mary's supporters was still raging, Rogers preached at the same place. His message was confined exclusively to an exposition of the gospel for the day and demonstrated moderate and sound judgement. Rogers was never deliberately offensive, nor did he use the pulpit as an opportunity to show any partisan or political bias. When necessary he was firm in his stand for truth and boldly denounced abuses and wickedness, even in high places, so he could never be accused of weakness or cowardice; but in this sermon he judged rightly that any attack on Mary on that holy day would be ill-timed and uncalled for, and so restricted himself to preaching the plain gospel.

It is also almost certain that he had not consented to the enthronement of Lady Jane, and that he conscientiously believed in the right of Mary's succession, although he knew that such an event would be catastrophic for the Reformation. However, it was offence enough in the eyes of some for him to succeed Ridley at Paul's Cross and to be recognized by the Council as one of its ablest preachers. Coupled with the fear of him that the Catholics already entertained on account of his boldness and ability, this sermon was sufficient for him to become a marked man.

Rogers's second sermon

On 19 July, Mary, who was passionately loyal to the memory of Catherine of Aragon, her rejected Catholic Spanish mother, was proclaimed queen in London amidst 'bell ringing, blazes and shouts of applause', and Lady Jane's brief reign was at an end. According to Geoffrey Elton, Mary's 'triumphant success owed everything to her being King Henry's daughter and very little to her Catholic faith'.

Mary arrived in London on 3 August and the following Sunday (6th) Rogers, who knew the probable consequences of his message, again preached at Paul's Cross. He delivered a godly and vehement sermon, avowing and confirming the doctrines he and others had taught in Edward's days, exhorting the congregation to be steadfast in gospel truth and warning them against 'all pestilent Popery, idolatry and superstition'. He severely condemned the misuses that were made of the property of the suppressed abbeys and the confiscated goods of the churches, which infuriated the guilty parties, who demanded that he be called to account for his comments.

No fear

When he stood up to preach there was no wavering or timidity, no effort to wriggle out of the Council's command, no shirking from his responsibilities, even though he knew that every word he spoke was only adding to the future terrors of his condemnation. How different was this sermon to the last one he had given in the same place! Then he had mildly preached the gospel and sent his hearers away either mourning over their sins or comforted in their great salvation. Now he was no longer the pastor instructing his flock, but the accuser of a vile and angry priesthood into whose hands he saw had already been committed the future direction of the government. The language he used was strong and incendiary as he pronounced judgement on the hypocrites.

What if he had failed to speak out? What if he had compromised his message and through physical timidity and moral weakness played along with his enemies? What a blow would have been inflicted on the blessed gospel and how his example would have deterred others from standing for the truth! 'There never was any position in the whole history of the Reformation, all things considered, where the responsibilities thrown upon a single man were greater and the results more important, or where they were more nobly sustained. Surely, his conduct was more than noble—it was magnificent!' It was as a result of this sermon that Rogers ended his career as a minister of the gospel and began to tread the path to martyrdom.

His defence

The outcome of that sermon was predictable. He was summoned before the same Privy Council that had ordered him to preach and asked to explain his sermon. He defended himself so ingeniously that they were compelled, for the time being, to dismiss him unharmed. It seems that his defence consisted of a simple appeal to the fact that the Protestant religion was still recognized and protected by the law of the land, for nothing had yet been repealed. The Council could not answer his arguments and therefore had no alternative but to set him free.

He referred to this trial in the papers he wrote after his final examinations and declared that 'never a Catholic of them all did ever so much therein as he did' to check the abuses he had mentioned in his sermon, and nor would he or others who contended against the same be charged by God with neglect of duty in that respect. Once again the strength of his character stands out and his determination not to overlook what he regarded as grave religious errors or ungodly conduct.

This was Rogers's last sermon and, according to his own testimony, his last public address of any kind; for, at his examination, when Gardiner failed to sustain his charge that he had then preached against the queen, the accuser fell back on the assertion that Rogers had subsequently read his lectures in St Paul's. Rogers immediately replied, 'That did I not; let that be proved, and let me die for it!' He had been unsparing in his denunciations of the Popish religion and its upholders in the church and state, but he had not attacked the queen, of whom he held a better opinion than many of his class.

Old St Paul's Cathedral and St Paul's Cross

Later, during his second examination, Rogers said that he asked Gardiner why he had sent him to prison. Gardiner replied because he had preached against the queen. He answered, 'That is not so, and I would be bound to prove and to stand the trial of the law, that no man should be able to prove it, and thereupon would set my life. I preached a sermon at Paul's Cross, after the queen went to the Tower, but said nothing against the queen. I call the large audience as my witness. You, after my examination, had let me go free after the preaching of that sermon.'

Rogers also replied to Gardiner, when he professedly offered him the mercy of the queen, saying, 'I never offended, nor was disobedient to her grace; yet will I not refuse her mercy.' It was proved that he was only going to be shown mercy if he acknowledged the Pope to be the head of the church, a singular method of compromising a political offence, if, as has been alleged by some, Rogers was regarded as a political offender.

Why was Rogers asked to preach again?
But why was Rogers asked by the Council, already 'overmatched with Popish bishops', to be the *first* to preach a public sermon after the queen's arrival in London, although it was not his regular day for that duty, for he had preached at the Cross only three weeks before, and it was customary for the principal clergy to officiate there in rotation? The answer is obvious: because of their undisguised hatred of him. They had commanded this sermon with the express hope of entrapping him, or at least of compelling him to define his future position. But Rogers had already foreseen the results of Mary's accession and had counted the cost for his opposition. He knew the course he was going to pursue. Even at that day he saw in the dim distance the burning stake that was going to be the goal of his career.

Rogers must have carefully thought about life, liberty, his loving family and the chance to escape abroad, but nothing persuaded him to put down the cross of Christ. He had returned to England at the call of duty and he was not about to forsake that call now. Even at this time he had resolved what he was later to tell the sheriff on the morning of his execution, that what he had preached he would seal with his blood.

Queen Mary and Gilbert Bourne

The new queen came to the throne determined to purge her realm of what she considered to be heresy, to restore England to papal obedience and to 'save her country from mortal sin'. Even as she was on her way to London, her religious policy, which needed no explanation, was being eagerly if illegally implemented by squires and clergy across the country. In many places of the realm, 'priests were commanded by Catholic lords and knights to say mass in Latin with consecration and elevation of the body and blood of Christ under the form of bread and wine with a decent order'.

Mary's first public act on reaching London was to issue a proclamation announcing her inability 'to hide that religion which God and the world knows she has ever professed from her infancy' and allowing and encouraging (not compelling at this stage) her subjects to follow her example. Inevitably her determination would mean reconciliation to Rome and the restoration of laws passed by parliament 150 years earlier that imposed the death penalty on anyone who rejected the teaching of the Roman Catholic Church. Suspected heretics would be tried by a bishop's court and, if found guilty, they would be urged to recant. If they refused, they would be burned to death.

Mary lost no time in surrounding herself with counsellors and ministers of her own religious persuasion, and although she assured the Protestants she would make no changes to the then lawfully established religion, measures were implemented and preparations made for the crushing of the Reformers and the Reformation and the restoration of the Papacy throughout England. Gardiner and Bonner were restored to their sees, Winchester and London respectively, and the former was made chancellor, and practically became the queen's prime minister. The Marquis of Winchester was allowed to retain his post of treasurer, but relatively few of her brother's advisers remained members of her Council.

Gilbert Bourne

On Saturday 12 August, Mary summoned the magistrates of London and declared to them that she did not intend to put any restraint on her subjects, but designed to have them instructed in the 'true religion' by 'godly, virtuous and learned preachers', and that through their teaching they would be led to agree with her religious sentiments.

The man selected to start these public instructions was Gilbert Bourne, who had received a prebend at St Paul's in 1545 and four years later had become rector of High Ongar in Essex and archdeacon of Bedford. He became chaplain to Bonner in the reign of Henry VIII and preached against heretics. He stood by Bonner during the hearing of his appeal in 1549 and on Mary's accession he acted as one of the delegates for Bonner's restitution.

Even if the queen had tried, she could not have picked a man more obnoxious to the Protestants or fit to perform her odious tasks. Bourne was a man of considerable ability, who had abandoned his Protestant principles to become one of the Reformation's fiercest persecutors. He was in great favour throughout Mary's reign, and became bishop of Bath and Wells in 1554, in which capacity he sat as one of Rogers's judges. Immediately after his consecration he commissioned Cottrel, his vicar-general, to deprive and punish 'all in holy orders keeping in adulterous embraces women upon show of feigned and pretended matrimony' and 'married laics who in pretence and under colour of priestly orders had rashly and unlawfully mingled themselves in ecclesiastical rights'. As a result there were eighty-two cases of deprivation.

During the reign of Elizabeth he refused to take the oaths of supremacy and allegiance and with six other bishops was committed to the Tower. When the plague struck London in 1562 he was removed from the Tower for fear of infection, but remained a prisoner at large until his death at Silverton, Devon, on 10 September 1569.

Bourne's sermon

On Sunday 13 August 1553, Bourne stood in the same place at St Paul's Cross where Rogers had ended his public preaching a week before. There was a sizeable congregation, including the lord mayor and other city officials, Bonner and a large number of Protestants, among whom were

Rogers and John Bradford. His chosen subject was the gospel of the day, but he paid little attention to it, preferring to praise his master Bonner, abuse King Edward, the Protestants and the recognized religion of the land. His language was so offensive that the Protestants became increasingly agitated and finally enraged. Stones and other missiles were thrown at him, and at length a dagger, from which he narrowly escaped a serious injury. Bourne did not have the courage to continue in the storm he had raised, but his intended end had been accomplished, for the Protestants' riotous behaviour had given the authorities sufficient excuse to deal severely with them.

Bourne quietly slipped down from the pulpit, leaving his harangue unfinished. His brother and other priests with him in the pulpit were obliged to humble themselves so far as to urge Bradford, whose sleeve the thrown dagger had touched, to speak to the angry crowd. After a few words from Bradford the protestors were pacified. He called to Rogers and together they escorted Bourne unmolested through the crowd, remaining with him until he reached a place of safety.

On the very same day as the uproar the queen's Council was in session at the Tower. Either they were waiting for the outcome of Bourne's verbal attack, or they were called together immediately the news of the tumult reached the queen or her ministers. In the *Journal* of the Council for that day there appears the following entry: 'They be ordered, every alderman in his ward, severally, to send forthwith for the curates of every parish church within their liberties, and to warn them not only to forbear to preach, or make any open or solemn reading of the Scripture in their churches, unless the said preachers be such as be specially licensed thereto by the queen's highness.' Three days after Bourne's sermon Bradford was arrested and during his trial the next year he was falsely accused of stirring up the crowd at the Cross to riot. In his defence he dismissed such accusations and rather spoke of the help he had given Bourne, but his explanation was rejected.

Two proclamations

The above note and Gardiner's recognition of the need for caution in the queen's religious policy, appears to have been the germ of Mary's first proclamation that was publicly issued on 18 August, and which had the appearance of 'friendly advice' from the queen to her people. She assured them that she had no intention of disturbing their enjoyment of their own religion, but appealed to all men everywhere to embrace the 'ancient religion'. After warning the two parties against reviling each other as idolaters or heretics, she promised that disputes in religion would be settled by common consent, meaning in parliament. At the same time the proclamation positively prohibited all preaching and reading of the Scriptures by Protestants, as determined by the Council the previous Sunday.

On Monday 21 August another proclamation was published, by which every Protestant was prohibited from reasoning against or even discussing the actions of the queen and Council, whatever they might be. Both these edicts had no moral or legal value and could only be maintained by force. The Protestants, being the weaker party, had to submit.

A few weeks later Mary revealed her true colours when she secretly received a visit from a disguised Francesco Commendone, chamberlain to Pope Julius III. Mary told him she wanted to restore to her realm the papal supremacy as well as Catholic worship, and gave him an autographed letter to the Pope. She was told that the Pope had already designated Cardinal Pole as papal legate in England. In reply the queen asked that he might come to her as soon as possible.

With these opening measures the queen was gradually tightening the screw on the Protestants and making it more difficult for them to follow the 'religion of the Reformers'.

Arrested

The Council did not even wait for the formality of publicly issuing the proclamations before putting their plan into operation. On 16 August, two days before the first edict appeared, although three days after it had been written, Rogers, who had been silent for the last ten days since preaching at Paul's Cross, was again summoned to appear before the Council at the Tower. He had already been tried for the 'crime' and acquitted and yet that did not stop these despisers of true religion from accosting him a second time. The only flimsy excuse that has been offered for this disregard of the law is that the ease with which Bradford and Rogers had calmed the tumult on the occasion of Bourne's preaching was 'proof' that they had been the instigators of it.

Rogers placed under house arrest

The lords of the Council, who 'desired his blood', argued with him concerning his doctrine and then ordered him to stay as a prisoner in his own house (that is, his official residence), to which he agreed, although by ignoring their command, he could easily have escaped their cruel hands. He certainly had reasons enough to run, but he was determined to stand up for Christ's cause and to defend the truth even if it meant endangering his life.

In this first official proceeding against Rogers, particular pains were taken to identify him with the 'Thomas Matthew' of the 1537 Bible. The Council's minutes of this meeting read as follows: 'John Rogers, *alias* Matthew, a seditious preacher, ordered by the lords of the Council to keep himself as prisoner in his house at Paul's, without conference of any person other than such as are daily with him in [his] household, until such time as he has contrary commandment.'

Why was Rogers not imprisoned immediately?

Interestingly, other men who were arrested on the same day were immediately committed to crowded and filthy prisons in accordance with the usual custom. So why was Rogers dealt with so leniently? He was not even asked to give his word that he would not attempt to escape. For the next six months he was allowed relative freedom within the confines of his house, enjoyed constant communication with his family, and was not even guarded to prevent him from leaving his home, town or country.

The answer seems to be that as Rogers was both a scholar and a leader among the Reformers, the papal hierarchy feared him. His moderation, command of temper and wise judgement, coupled with courage and religious zeal, made him a dangerous foe, who had to be dealt with most carefully. His imprisonment would have been a weak punishment for such a man and would not have fulfilled their evil designs. Besides, they did not have sufficient grounds for making him a state prisoner. Rogers had recognized the sovereignty of the queen even while he zealously preached against what she believed, and the Council knew he had the right to preach so long as the Act establishing his own religion had not been legally repealed.

No doubt they were also hoping he would be influenced by his family and friends to attempt an escape. Then they could pour scorn on his name and supposed faithfulness to his cause, which in turn might shake the weaker members of the Protestant faith and even tempt them to follow their champion abroad.

At this point it seems that the entire responsibility for upholding the Reformers' cause rested on Rogers's shoulders. Many like-minded men had already fled the country, while others were incarcerated in various prisons, where they had little opportunity to assist in the battle and simply waited for their expected execution. Only Rogers enjoyed comparative freedom in the midst of bitter enemies, who were restrained by motives of policy from instantly taking his life.

Reasons to escape

From a human point of view there were many reasons for Rogers to escape. He had a large family to support, who would be destitute if he could not provide for them. He could return to his old charge in Germany, where he might live for many years and pursue a useful ministry. He was not very old and so had many years before him in which to glorify his Saviour. Under house arrest there was little hope of being able to preach the gospel or of doing much good in England.

But he dismissed all these reasons, for he was a man of integrity whose

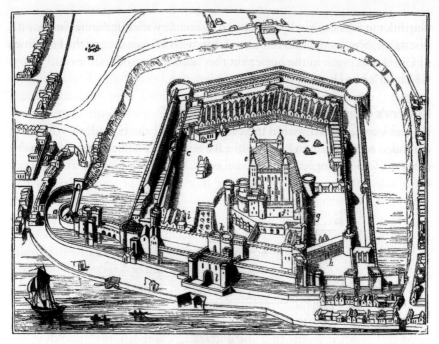

The Tower of London

Christian principles were higher and holier than thoughts of personal comfort and safety. He determined to stay and stand, and regarded escape as little less than apostasy. He knew his life was in the hand of God and not in the hand of his persecutors, and that God would use him in whatever way he saw fit. He had no thought or desire of averting the responsibilities that were laid on him. So, to the great disappointment and frustration of his enemies, he remained a 'prisoner in his own house' and calmly waited for the next scene in his drama to unfold.

However, he was prepared to allow his family and friends to resort to any proper means to secure his release while remaining obedient to the authorities set over him. In his own words, he later said to Gardiner, 'I was almost half a year in my house, where I was obedient to you, God knows it, and *spoke with no man*.' His wife did all in her power to obtain his liberty. On one occasion she, along with eight female friends, paid a visit to

Gardiner at his house in Richmond to intercede with him for her husband's discharge. She visited him either on Christmas Day or during the festivities of Christmas week in the hope that the 'season of good will' would soften Gardiner's hard heart. Her mission failed.

Rogers's official residence

Rogers was confined within the cathedral close, the boundaries of which extended on one side to Paternoster Row and Ave Maria Lane and on the other to Old Change, Carter Lane and Creed Lane. Within these limits

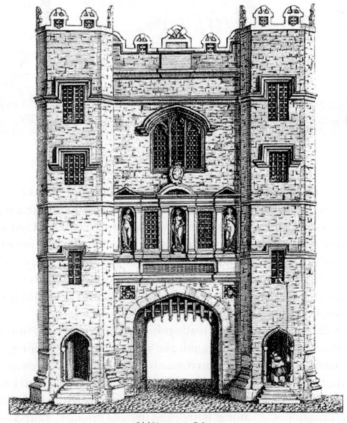

Old Newgate Prison

were various buildings for the use and occupancy of the bishop of London and the other cathedral dignitaries. One of these buildings was assigned to Rogers as his official residence. It was close to Bonner's house, which was situated in the angle formed by Paternoster Row and Ave Maria Lane. During the time he was detained Rogers was deprived of the income from his various livings, but not of the livings themselves; for although Thomas Chetham (or Chetteham) was collated to the prebend of St Pancras on 10 October 1553, no one was appointed to succeed him in the vicarage of St Sepulchre until 11 February 1555, when George Bullock was instituted, just one week after Rogers had been burned in Smithfield.

His confinement left his wife and children in desperate need and in his bold declaration to Gardiner he said that he had been dealt with most cruelly and unlawfully, both by placing and keeping him in confinement, at great cost and charges, and in depriving him of the means to pay those charges and to support his family.

Transferred to Newgate prison

He remained in his house as a prisoner until at the instigation of Bonner, bishop of London, who could not stand to have such honest neighbours living near him, he was removed to Newgate prison, by then a 'horridly loathsome' prison, on Saturday 27 January 1554. He was placed among thieves and murderers. Bonner had tried for a long time to achieve this end and eventually succeeded with the authority of Gardiner. Both these men manifested a consistent and persevering malignity towards Rogers, more so it seems than to any other of the Reformers. What transpired between Rogers and his adversaries over the next year is not wholly known, except what is learned from his examinations, which he wrote down.

Rogers was not a political prisoner

As has been said before, Rogers was not a political prisoner, although he has been described as a 'demagogue and seditious person'. His opponents failed to establish his connection with any of the political movements of the day and in his own dying testimony he declared never to have spoken against the queen or her authority. The original sentence of condemnation, passed on Rogers by Gardiner, is proof positive of this fact. That document says he was 'accused and detected, and notoriously slandered of, *heresy*', not some political offence. The tribunal found that he had 'taught, held and affirmed, and obstinately defended divers *errors, heresies* and *damnable opinions, contrary to the doctrine and determination of the holy Church*'. He was certainly not condemned for treasonable opinions concerning the queen or the civil government. When Gardiner attempted to hint at treason, Rogers immediately and indignantly defied him to prove it and no more was heard on the matter. Nor was he ever accused of causing or tried concerning the tumult at Paul's Cross on the occasion of Bourne's preaching there. His offence was clearly a religious one.

The two main 'heresies' of which he was accused were 'that the Catholic Church of Rome is the church of antichrist' and 'that, in the sacrament of the altar, there is not, substantially and really, the natural body and blood of Christ'. These are the only charges on which he was tried, found guilty and condemned and he never denied them. Gardiner declared him to be guilty of '*heretical pravity* and *execrable doctrine*' and finally condemned him 'as guilty of the most detestable *heresies*, and as an obstinate, impenitent sinner, refusing penitently to return to the lap and unity of the holy mother Church'.

Bonner's hatred of Rogers

The real cause of Bonner's hatred of Rogers was his own inherent selfishness and his adversary's connection with Nicholas Ridley. Bonner despised Ridley, because he had occupied his seat in the see of London, and opposed his subordinates, who filled stalls or other offices in the cathedral. He knew Rogers was in Ridley's administration and thus occupied a post that used to be held by one of his own minions, the control of which he could not regain until Rogers had been legally deprived of it. To put it bluntly: Rogers was in his way and had to be removed.

He also perhaps attributed to him, as one of the leading Reformers during Edward's reign, some blame for his own deprivation and imprisonment in 1549, and he was not a man to forget an injury, but revenged himself whenever he had the opportunity 'a thousand fold'. In addition, he recognized in Rogers a man of ability and influence as a religious opponent and, for the sake of his own church, was eager that so wise a counsellor and so powerful a debater should be permanently silenced. If he had had the chance, he would have brought about his death much earlier, but was compelled to submit to the policy of his superiors, who still hoped Rogers would flee abroad.

Gardiner's hatred of Rogers

The comments made above also apply to some extent to Gardiner, but it is nearer the truth to say that he was always a bitter and unrelenting enemy of anyone who had anything to do with the translation, publication or distribution of the English Scriptures. When the Matthew's Bible was issued in 1537 he was in France, but after his return in the latter part of 1538 he did all in his power to prevent its further circulation. Rogers, from his connection with it, made himself the hated foe of Gardiner, and as soon as he was restored to power under Mary, he singled out Rogers for persecution, knowing full well that as Lord Chancellor, he would eventually preside at his trial and condemnation. At the trial of Rogers he added to his real name the *alias* Matthew, an evident indication that at least one of his offences lay in the work he had performed under that name.

The hatred of these men continued after they had consigned Rogers to the most loathsome prison in London. The restrictions they imposed on him and the severities he endured far exceeded those suffered by other prisoners. However, he made no complaint, but bore his hardships manfully, even 'merrily'.

Articles of faith

Q ueen Mary was crowned on 1 October 1553 and her first parliament assembled four days later. To allay apprehensions a modest programme was submitted to it. The queen was declared to have been born 'in a most just and lawful matrimony'; the Edwardian Act of Uniformity was repealed, thus restoring the form of worship used in the last year of Henry VIII's reign, although, with the heresy laws repealed by Somerset not being re-enacted, the state did not yet assist in the enforcement of Catholic orthodoxy which Mary and Gardiner wanted to enforce.

On 18 October Mary caused bishops and other church dignitaries to meet in St Paul's, London, which finally broke on the queen's command on 13 December. Two items were first discussed: the forty-two articles of a catechism that had been published shortly before Edward's death, and 'a very abominable' *Book of Common Prayer*, which was successfully outlawed in time for Christmas. The

Mary Tudor

catechism was described as 'pestiferous and full of heresies' and of being put on 'the last synod fraudulently and therefore the present synod must disown it'. One of the main issues centred on the natural presence of Christ in the sacrament.

John Philpot

John Philpot, then archdeacon of Winchester, was the chief defender of the catechism. In his speech on 19 October he urged that the authors and publishers of that work should be allowed to come before convocation on its behalf and particularly desired that 'Ridley and Rogers, and two or three more' should have a similar privilege, regarding it as unfair that a work should be condemned without a defence from its supporters. This proposition was rejected, as the persons named were still too powerful among the people to make this concession safe.

With force and clarity Philpot, with a few others, defended the truth of the gospel against its enemies; and although the queen had given to all the members 'full liberty of speech', he was treated shamefully. He was called to account before Gardiner, who examined and condemned him. It must be said that it was for Philpot's firm refusal to sign the document that branded a catechism, which had both truth and synodal authority on its side, as heretical, as much as for his resistance to transubstantiation and the mass, which led to his punishment. He was excommunicated 'as contumacious', without any personal citation, illegally deprived of his archdeaconry, and committed to the King's Bench prison in Borough High Street, Southwark.

Debates

In the early months of 1554 Cranmer, Latimer and Ridley were moved from the Tower to Oxford to dispute publicly with the 'theological gladiators of the two universities, who hoped to discredit them openly to the shame and disgrace of all Protestants'. Heresy was the charge levied against them. They had little or no time to prepare, for at first they thought they were being led to their trial and execution, and were only allowed to take with them the books they could carry. The trial began on 14 April at St Mary's Church. Gardiner had drawn up three articles that dealt with the

Mass to which each prisoner was to subscribe. The men were brought in separately, but they all denied the articles. On Friday 20 April they were given a final chance to submit and when they refused were declared heretics and excommunicated.

Diarmaid MacCulloch describes this disputation as 'unusually hysterical, both among the Catholic participants and the packed audiences' and the 'moderator did not make much effort to control it'. He agrees with Foxe and his Victorian editors when they say that 'much of the technical framing of the arguments was fairly shoddy by the standards of university logic at the time'. Although the Catholics claimed to win a significant victory, no official version of the proceedings was published.

Elated at their supposed success of making it appear that the Protestant champions had been fairly defeated by theological argument, the Catholic leaders tried to involve other eminent Protestant leaders in a similar disgrace, and in the latter part of the same month or at the beginning of May, it was proposed that Rogers, Hooper, Bradford and others should be sent to Cambridge to take part in another debate. A confidential messenger from these men was sent to Oxford to find out from Cranmer, Latimer and Ridley whether or not it was their duty to obey the summons to dispute at Cambridge. Ridley did not give any decisive counsel but said that he could not blame them if they declined, for they could not expect justice. However, it was possible they might consider appearing if they thought their hearers might profit from their arguments.

Hooper urged them to refuse unless the original authors their opponents were going to quote were brought forward, and unless the reporters were placed under the obligation of an oath to give a true statement of what was uttered. They were also advised to break off the disputation in the middle if they thought any secret conferences were being employed or contemptuous language used by their opponents, and to appeal for a hearing before the queen.

Their defence

After due consideration, these men decided not to take part in such a discussion on the grounds that the tribunal, before whom they would have to appear, would not be impartial and therefore more harm than good would be done to their cause. So that their decision was not interpreted as either cowardice or lukewarmness, they drew up and signed a paper detailing the reasons for their refusal and recounting certain articles of faith.

It is plain from their paper that these men regarded the clergy *only* as their enemies. Rogers may have dreaded Mary's accession and its probable results, but he admitted her right to the throne. He seems to have discriminated between her and her civil advisers and those to whom she entrusted the spiritual concerns of the realm. He was unwilling to trust himself and his cause to the mercy of the Catholic doctors, but was prepared to cast himself on the justice of the queen, her Council and even the whole parliament.

John Hooper

Secondly, it is apparent from the declarations in this paper that these men were confined 'not as rebels, traitors, seditious persons, thieves or transgressors of any laws of this realm, inhibitions, proclamations or commandments of the queen's highness, or of any of the Council's (God's name be praised therefore), but alone for the conscience [they had] to God and his most holy word and truth, on most certain knowledge'.

Reasons for refusal

These men were only prepared to dispute by writing, unless they were before the queen's highness and her Council or before the parliament house, for the following reasons:

1. Because it is known to the whole world that the determination of both the universities in matters of religion, especially in the area in dispute, are directly against God's word; and that they be our open enemies and have already condemned our causes before any disputation has taken place.
2. Because the prelates and clergy do not seek either us or the truth, but our destruction and their glory.
3. Because the censors and judges are manifest enemies to the truth, and that which is worse, obstinate enemies before whom pearls are not to be cast.
4. Because some of us have been in prison these eight or nine months, where we have had no books, no paper, no pen, no ink or convenient place to study; and we should do evil to dispute with them who may allege the fathers and their testimonies, because our memories have not that which we have recently read to reprove what they shall report and wrest from the authors to their purpose, or to bring forth what would be to our advantage.
5. Because in disputation we shall not be permitted to prosecute our arguments, but shall be stopped when we would speak.
6. Because the notaries who shall receive and write the disputation shall be of their appointment and therefore do not or dare not favour the truth, and therefore must write either to please them, or else the judges and censors at their pleasure will put to and take from what is written by the notaries.

They addressed these reasons to the 'whole congregation and Church of England' and then said 'humbly requiring, and in the bowels of our Saviour Jesus Christ, beseeching all that fear God to behave themselves as obedient subjects to the queen's highness and the superior powers, which are ordained of God under her; rather, after our example, to give their heads to the block, than in any point to rebel or once to mutter against the Lord's anointed, we mean our sovereign lady, Queen Mary, into whose heart we beseech the Lord of mercy plentifully to pour the wisdom and grace of his Holy Spirit, now and for ever, Amen'. This is certainly not the language and advice of rebellious, seditious or even politically disaffected men.

Articles of faith

Their confession consisted of eight main points (summarized below), which they were confident, by God's grace, of being able to prove from Scripture:

1. We confess and believe all the Canonical books of the Old Testament and all the books of the New Testament to be the very true word of God and to be written by the inspiration of the Holy Spirit, and therefore to be heard accordingly, as the judge in all controversies and matters of religion.
2. We confess and believe the catholic church (which is the spouse of Christ) as the most obedient and loving wife, to embrace and follow the doctrine of these books in all matters of religion, and therefore is she to be heard accordingly.
3. We believe and confess all the articles of faith and doctrine in the Apostles' Creed and in the symbols of the councils of Nice, Constantinople, Ephesus, Chalcedon and Toletum (modern-day Toledo), and also Athanasius, Irenaeus, Tertullian, and Damasus.
4. We believe and confess concerning justification that it comes only from God's mercy through Christ by faith only.
5. We confess and believe concerning the exterior service of God that it ought to be according to the word of God, and therefore in the public congregation to be performed in an edifying language and not in Latin.
6. We confess and believe that God only by Christ Jesus is to be prayed to and called on.

7. We confess and believe that as a man departs this life so shall he be judged in the last day generally and enter into a state of the blessed for ever or damned for ever.

8. We confess and believe the sacraments of Christ, which are baptism and the Lord's Supper, that they ought to be ministered according to the institution of Christ.

Just before the close of the document, to reinforce what they had already said, they declared:

In the mean season, as obedient subjects, we shall behave ourselves towards all that be in authority, and not cease to pray to God for them, that he would govern them all, generally and particularly, with the spirit of wisdom and grace; and so we heartily desire and humbly pray all men to do, in no point consenting to any kind of rebellion or sedition against our sovereign lady, the queen's highness, but, where they cannot obey but they must disobey God, there to submit themselves, with all patience and humility, to suffer as the will and pleasure of the higher powers shall adjudge.

This confession was undersigned by twelve men, one of whom was John Rogers. These men wrote so clearly because they knew that their enemies would try to misinterpret and distort what they had written and even accuse them of writing purely to produce a temporary effect.

A prison petition

R ogers's confinement was very strict and he was not allowed to use his books or to write, although he managed to pen various documents secretly. Some of his fellow prisoners wrote a great deal while in prison and these writings have been preserved, but not a line has come down to succeeding generations from the pen of Rogers, except his own account of his examinations.

During these examinations he mentioned writing two 'supplications' or petitions to Gardiner while in Newgate, which, if they made it through the prison gate, were ignored. He also spoke of sending for his wife many times, probably to urge her to petition the authorities to curtail his harsh treatment; and, knowing what his likely fate was to be, he wanted to give her the counsel and instructions she needed before he died. He may have occasionally seen his wife, but for a long time before his death he had no communication with or knowledge of his family. He adds that John Gosnold and other friends endeavoured earnestly, but without success, to obtain from the Lord Chancellor some alleviation of his sufferings; and that he had heard some 'general things', probably about the progress of the Reformation, at the table while eating his meals, in all likelihood from the prison attendants, who casually spoke in his presence. These are the only instances in which he had any communication with the outside world or any knowledge of what was happening beyond the prison walls.

Petition of the preachers in prison

The only other publication with which Rogers was connected during his time in Newgate was a well-written petition, attributed principally to Bradford, which was probably presented to parliament from the preachers then in the various prisons. It is addressed to 'the king [Philip of Spain] and queen most excellent majesties, and to their most honourable and high court of parliament' and referred to Mary's third parliament that met in November 1554, in which the old heresy laws were re-enacted and 'ferocious new treason laws passed', as well as the repeal of all the anti-papal and anti-ecclesiastical legislation passed since 1529. It was written soon after November, as the men who signed it stated that they had been confined for fifteen or sixteen months. The first arrests had been made about the middle of August 1553.

The writers—Hooper, Ferrar, Taylor, Bradford, Philpot, Rogers and Saunders—claimed to have been loyal and obedient subjects to Edward VI and to have ministered God's word faithfully and sincerely; but, they say, 'contrary to all laws of justice, equity and right, we are in very extreme manner, not only cast into prison … but our livings also, our houses and possessions, our goods and books taken from us, and we are slandered to be most heinous heretics, our enemies themselves being both witnesses, accusers and judges, belying, slandering and misreporting your said subjects at their pleasure; whereas your said subjects being straightly kept in prison, cannot yet be suffered to come forth and make answer accordingly'.

They asked to be 'granted liberty, either by mouth or writing, in the plain English tongue, to answer before you, or indifferent arbiters to be appointed by your majesties, to such articles of controversy in religion as our said adversaries have already condemned us of heinous heresies. Provided that all things may be done with such moderation and quiet behaviour, as becomes subjects and children of peace, and that your said subjects may have the free use of all their own books and conference together among themselves.

'Which thing being granted, we doubt not but it shall plainly appear that we are true and faithful Christians, and neither heretics, neither teachers of heresy, nor cut off from the true catholic universal church of Christ.'

If these men were not able to prove that the doctrine of the church, homilies and service taught and set forth in the time of Edward VI was the true doctrine of Christ's catholic church and agreeable to the articles of the Christian faith, they stood ready to offer themselves 'to the most heavy punishment that it shall please your majesty to appoint'.

If the petition reached parliament, which in itself is doubtful, it was rejected by the enemies of the gospel, who were too busy reviving the old laws against heresy and in creating new ones with which to condemn the Reformers to pay it any regard. In December parliament was already setting in motion the re-enactment of these old laws, including the infamous Act of 1401 ('on the burning of heretics'), which allowed suspected heretics to be arrested and tried by their bishop in accordance with canon law. If the bishop found them guilty of heresy, they were to be handed over to the secular powers to be burned to death. The bill received the royal assent on 16 January 1555 at the end of the parliamentary session. Nineteen days later Rogers was burned at the stake.

Gardiner and Bonner

uring the eighteen months between the first arrests of the Protestants and their trials and condemnation, the Catholics were slowly but surely confirming their control of the affairs of church and state. Stephen Gardiner, with determination, had climbed to eminence and with his new found power and the queen's support moved swiftly to strike what he hoped would be a deathblow to the work and lives of the Reformers.

Gardiner's life

It is important to understand something of the life and character of Gardiner as he played such an important and decisive role in the examinations and condemnation of Rogers. Gardiner was educated in civil and canon law at Cambridge University and in the 1520s joined Cardinal Wolsey's service. He was poached by Henry VIII in 1529 to serve as his principal secretary and because of his tireless efforts to secure his divorce from Catherine of Aragon, which of course secured the king's

Stephen Gardiner

favour, he was rewarded with the bishopric of Winchester, the wealthiest see in England.

However, the fickle Henry became suspicious of Gardiner after he drafted the clergy's reply to the *Supplication against the Ordinaries*, and appointed Thomas Cranmer as archbishop of Canterbury. In order to regain favour with the king, Gardiner published a treatise that attacked the papacy. His *Episcopi de vera obedientia oratio* (*Bishop's speech on true obedience*) supported the king's supremacy as leader of the Church of England; yet, in keeping with the reputation for double dealing that dogged his career, only four years later he sided with the conservatives in their support of Roman Catholicism and led them in passing the Act of the Six Articles (1539), which required Englishmen to uphold the beliefs of the Roman Catholic Church. His 'sanguinary temper' came to the fore in the Six Articles, known as the 'bloody statute' or 'the bloody whip with six strings' by many Protestants, and on which so many deniers of the 'real presence' were executed. After Cromwell's downfall, Gardiner was appointed to replace him as chancellor of the university and Henry placed him on his royal Council as a means of quashing Protestant sympathisers.

He was imprisoned in the Tower during Edward's reign, but on Mary's arrival in London he was immediately released. On 23 August 1553 he was appointed Lord High Chancellor of the realm and in that capacity placed the crown on Mary's head at her coronation.

Gardiner died of the gout only about nine months after the execution of his first victim, which was in the eyes of many a 'just retribution'. 'I have sinned with Peter,' he exclaimed on his deathbed, 'but I have not wept with him,' which has been interpreted as 'an expression of his dying remorse for his repudiation of the Roman supremacy'.

Elton, in his work *England under the Tudors*, sums up his career:

He had played a prominent part in thirty-five years of public life without ever attaining to the power and influence he craved. Henry VIII distrusted him, Somerset and Northumberland feared him, Mary found him too English for her taste. Yet he had stood for a certain continuity and for a definite party of conservative patriots. He was very able, learned (especially in the canon and civil law), and energetic, but overbearing and violent in manner... His life achieved little, for even the continuity of the Anglican Church with pre-Reformation days owes more to Cranmer than to Gardiner.

Gardiner's character

Lloyd, in his *State Worthies*, says of Gardiner, 'He never did what he aimed at—never aimed at what he intended—never intended what he said—and never said what he thought: whereby he carried it so that others should do his business when they opposed it, and he should undermine theirs when he seemed to promote it. A man that was to be traced like a fox; and read, like the Hebrew, backward: if you would know what he did, you must observe what he did not.'

Foss in *Judges of England* remarks, 'With every desire to give impartial consideration to the arguments of those who attempt to palliate his conduct, it is impossible to acquit him of *originating* the laws which authorized these cruel measures [actually, the burning of 'heretics' was the execution of a law that Mary had reinstated], and of *carrying them into effect* with their extremist severity; and, conscientious as some may think him in his zeal for ancient Church, none but the most bigoted can justify the measures he adopted for its restoration.' Lord Campbell in *Lives of the Lord Chancellors* thinks his legal abilities and statesmanship are to be commended, but goes on to point out that he was supremely ambitious and 'displayed a *happy lubricity of conscience*, which surmounted or evaded every obstacle, convincing him that his duty coincided with his interest'.

'His malice,' comments Fuller, 'was like what is commonly said of white powder, which surely discharged the bullet, yet made no report, being secret in all his acts of cruelty. This made him often chide Bonner, calling him "ass", though not so much for killing poor people, as for not doing it more cunningly.'

Bonner

During Henry's reign, Edmund Bonner, bishop of London, in his zeal to implement the Act of the Six Articles, was responsible for the death of a fifteen-year-old boy, Richard Mekins, who had spoken against the sacrament. He was burned in Smithfield. Bonner also committed John Porter to prison for reading aloud from one of the six Bibles he had put in St Paul's Cathedral and making comments of his own in violation of the episcopal injunctions. Porter was fastened with a collar of iron to the wall of his dungeon and died within about a week. With such violent actions he struck fear into the heart of London's small but growing Protestant community.

The death of Henry proved a turning point in Bonner's career. Up to then he had submitted to the sovereign, supported him in the matter of his divorce, approved of the suppression of the monasteries, and taken the oath of Supremacy; but while accepting the break from Rome, he had always resisted the

Edmund Bonner (seated, right)

innovations of the Reformers and held tenaciously to the Catholic doctrines. Therefore, from the first he was opposed to the religious changes introduced by Somerset and Cranmer.

He was a leading opponent of the first Act of Uniformity and the *Book of Common Prayer* and when these became law he neglected to enforce them. On 1 September 1549, when he was required by the Council to maintain at St Paul's Cross that Edward's 'authority was as great during the minority as if he were thirty or forty years old', he refused, passing over the subject in silence. After being examined by Cranmer he was deprived of his bishopric and sent to the Marshalsea prison, where he remained till the accession of Mary.

After being restored to his see, Bonner visited his diocese and revived the mass and many practices and emblems of Catholic life, but the work was carried out slowly and with difficulty as the Reformers, particularly in London, strongly opposed the restoration of Catholic worship. Many street fights resulted from religious disputes and Bonner himself was physically attacked on at least two occasions. Mary's administration thought that the Reformers would best be dealt with by the ecclesiastical tribunals, rather than by the civil power, and on Bonner, as bishop of London, fell the chief burden to stamp out religious dissent. Therefore, in 1555 the persecutions for which he is notorious and that earned him the nickname *Bloody Bonner* commenced. The first victim, of course, was John Rogers.

Innocent or guilty?

On the one hand, his supporters claim that Bonner did not go out of his way to persecute; many of his victims were forced upon him by the king and queen, who at one point admonished him by letter 'not to dismiss the heretics brought before him so lightly as he and his brother bishops had done'. In truth, Mary's marriage basically handed over the government of England to Philip II of Spain and a severity towards heretics like that of the Spanish inquisition was inevitable. Bonner, it is claimed, was simply 'acting as an ecclesiastical sheriff in the most refractory district of the realm'.

On the other hand, his detractors point out that it was Bonner who brought it to pass that the condemnation and burning of heretics should be part of his ordinary official duties, and represent him as hounding men and women to death with merciless vindictiveness. During 1555 and the following three years burnings of heretics occurred all over England, but most frequently in Bonner's diocese of London.

There is no doubt that Bonner condemned many 'heretics' to the fire, and Richard Rex is right when he says that Bonner 'rejoiced in the unexpected chance to repay his enemies' and his actions were 'often personal rather than merely judicial'. His 'coarse liking for the task' must never be exonerated or excused, but the murderous policy was inspired by the queen, and even Bonner was driven on by orders from above. When a critical crowd gathered at one burning, Bonner produced a letter from the queen ordering him to stop procrastinating and get on with the job. Yes, it is true that he did not protest against the inhumane laws and was so hated that men would say of any ill-favoured fat fellow in the street, 'There goes Bonner', but the blame must be placed fairly and squarely at Mary's door for her unprecedented and violent persecutions.

Mary's third parliament

The third parliament after Mary's accession opened in November 1554. By that time Gardiner had brought together a group of men ready to carry out any measure that might be proposed. He had already effected the marriage of the queen with a foreign Catholic prince, abolished the English church service, and restored the authority of the Pope; now he turned his attention to the prisoners, of whom he intended to make such fearful examples as would check the progress of the Reformation, confirm his own power and advance the interests of his church. The first bill introduced at the opening of the session had reference to this object and nearly all the business transacted related to it.

When Cardinal Pole, as the Pope's legate, arrived in London, King Philip greeted him at Whitehall. When Mary met the Cardinal she claimed the child in her womb leapt as John the Baptist had done when the Virgin Mary greeted his mother Elizabeth. The pregnancy, however, proved to be false. On 30 November, Parliament convened 'for a

Reginald Pole

ceremony unique in parliamentary history, the granting of absolution for national schism through a nation's representative institution'. Gardiner, as Lord Chancellor, presented to Philip and Mary a petition for absolution, begging them in turn to present it to the cardinal. Pole had his papal authorization read out in full, and then solemnly and 'formally granted the kingdom absolution and freedom from all religious censure'. Parliament also passed Acts confirming the restoration of the papal power and the Council successfully recommended the full revival of the old penal laws against heresy.

Mary, who was easily persuaded that 'irreclaimable heretics' had to be punished with death, consented to the re-enactment of the statute originally passed against the Lollards in the reigns of Richard II, Henry IV and Henry V, which punished heresy at the stake, and to the restoration of the bishops' courts. Thus the great persecution, for which Mary earned the title among Protestants of 'that wicked Jezebel of England', was set in place. On 16 January 1555 Mary dissolved her third parliament, which had been in existence for only two months. Four days later the new laws took effect and two weeks after that John Rogers was burned at the stake.

The haste with which things moved against the Reformers underlines the anxiety of the Catholic leaders to begin their work of destruction. In fact, they had only waited for the formal announcement of legal authority in case more summary measures stirred up the opposition of the people. In truth, the laws under which they were about to act were *ex post facto* as far as the prisoners were concerned, for their restraint had prevented them from violating them; and the authorities were now too powerful to worry about any interference from the populace.

Rogers's first examination

Two days after the revived laws came into force, 22 January 1555, the first official proceedings were taken under them. At least eleven 'heretics' were brought on that day before Gardiner and the Privy Council, then sitting in the house of the former, near the church of St Mary Overie in Southwark. Those present officially were Gardiner, as presiding officer; the bishops of Durham, Ely and Worcester; the lords William Paget and William Howard; secretary Sir John Bourne; and Sir Richard Southwell, master general of the ordinance. It was a preliminary proceeding, the object of which was to see if any of the prisoners, after their long confinement, were ready to recant; but more especially it was designed to trap them into some sort of admission or declaration of their heresies, that could be used against them under the new laws.

The prisoners

Of all the prisoners brought before the Council with Rogers only the names of Hooper, Edward Crome and Harold Tomson are known. Crome was the rector of St Mary Aldermary in London and a preacher of some eminence. He had been in trouble for alleged heresies two or three times before, but always managed to escape with some trifling punishment. After Mary's accession he was again arrested (13 January 1554) for preaching without a licence and kept in the Fleet for a year before coming to trial with Rogers. Having had some practice 'in the art of recantation', he must have made sufficient compromises, for his life was spared, although he remained in prison until the accession of Elizabeth. He probably resumed preaching on his release as he held his old rectory when he died about 20 June 1562. He was buried in his own church, St Mary Aldermary.

There is no other reference to Tomson. As his name does not appear at any of the subsequent sessions, nor is he in any of the lists of martyrs from this time, it may be assumed that he was the other person mentioned by Rogers as being discharged through the influence of one of the Council, Lord William Howard.

Concerning his ten companions Rogers says that one of them, a citizen of London, yielded to the compliances demanded (Crome); and that the other (Tomson?), who was only required through the friendship of a member of the Council to respond affirmatively to the non-committal question whether he would be an honest man as his father had been before him, was immediately discharged. The remaining eight refused to receive the Cardinal's blessing or to acknowledge the authority of the Pope and so were sent back to prison.

Christ, the supreme head of the church

The first examination of John Rogers and the answers he made to the Lord Chancellor and to the rest of the Council took place on Tuesday 22 January 1555. As soon as the examination opened Gardiner abruptly intimated that he knew the object of the interview and demanded, if Rogers was willing, that he, there and then, abandon his old faith and acknowledge the Papal creed and authority. Interestingly, his enemies never spoke of the *Romish* or *Roman Catholic* Church; it was always just the *Catholic* Church.

Gardiner: Sir, you have heard of the state of the realm in which it now stands.

Rogers: No, my lord, I have been kept in prison and except there has been some general thing said at the dinner or supper table, I have heard nothing.

Gardiner replied in a mocking tone: General things, general things! You have heard of my lord cardinal [Pole's] coming, and that parliament [November 1554] has received his blessing, with only one man [Sir Ralph Bagnal] who spoke against it. Such unity and such a miracle have not been seen. And all of them, 160 in the house of commons, have with one assent received pardon for their offences, for the schism that we have had in England, in refusing the holy father of Rome to be head of the Catholic Church. How say you, are you content to unite and knit yourself to the faith of the Catholic Church with us in the state in which it is now in England? Will you do that?

Rogers: I never did nor will dissent from the catholic church.

Gardiner: But I speak of the state of the Catholic Church in which we stand now in England, having received the Pope to be supreme head.

Rogers: I know no other head but Christ of his catholic church; nor will I acknowledge the bishop of Rome to have any more authority than any other bishop has by the word of God, and by the doctrine of the old and pure catholic church 400 years after Christ.

Gardiner then taunted Rogers: Why did you then acknowledge King Henry VIII to be supreme head of the church, if Christ were the only head?

Gardiner imagined that he had ensnared his victim, for in the dedication to Henry VIII in the Matthew's Bible, Rogers had addressed the king as 'the chief and supreme head of the Church of England'.

Rogers, who was prepared for this objection, replied: I never granted him to have any supremacy in spiritual things, as are the forgiveness of sins, giving of the Holy Spirit, authority to be a judge above the word of God.

Gardiner: Yes, if you had said so in his days, you would not be alive now.

Other members of the Council, Cuthbert Tunstall, then bishop of Durham, and Nicholas Heath, the bishop of Worcester, nodded their heads at Rogers and laughed. Rogers denied their accusation and would have told them how Henry was meant to be the supreme head, but they looked at each other and laughed again and made such a noise that he was constrained to keep quiet.

The parliament of 1534

Gardiner said there was no problem in having Christ to be supreme head and also the bishop of Rome. When Rogers was about to answer that there could not be two heads of one church and to declare the vanity of such reasoning, Gardiner said, 'What do you say? Give us a direct answer whether you will be one of this Catholic Church or not, with us in the state in which we are now?'

Rogers: My lord, I cannot believe that you yourselves do think in your hearts that he is supreme head in forgiving of sins, seeing you and all the bishops of the realm have now for twenty years preached and some of you have also written to the contrary [Rogers was referring to Gardiner's treatise *De vera obedientia*, which was first published in 1535. This work argued for royal, rather than papal, supremacy of the English church. Marian Protestants frequently taunted Gardiner with his authorship of this work and, in fact, illicit Protestant presses reprinted the work during Mary's reign], and the parliament has so long ago agreed to it. [This was the parliament of 1534 that had abolished the authority of the Pope in the kingdom and declared Henry to be the supreme head of the church. Gardiner himself had, by a solemn oath, acknowledged this Act and sworn fidelity to its requirements.]

Gardiner, knowing the truth of what Rogers said, did not try to controvert it, but interrupted him and said, 'Tush, man! That parliament was with great cruelty constrained to abolish and put away the primacy from the bishop of Rome.' In other words, he claimed that he and the others had been compelled, by persecution, to appear to consent to what was really against their consciences.

Rogers promptly retorted: With cruelty? Why then I perceive that you take a wrong way with cruelty to persuade men's consciences. For it should appear by your doings now that the cruelty then used has not persuaded *your* consciences. How would you then have *our* consciences persuaded with cruelty? [This was a direct accusation of hypocrisy.]

Gardiner: I talk to you of no cruelty, but that they were so often and so cruelly called on in that parliament to let the Act go forward, yes and even with force driven thereto, whereas in this parliament it was so uniformly received.

William Paget, in the hope of creating a diversion, then told Rogers more plainly what Gardiner meant. Rogers had paid Paget no attention, probably indignant that a man, who had been one of the Councillors of the late king, should now be found actively persecuting the faith, which he had then pretended to uphold.

Rogers: Why then, my lord, what will you conclude thereby? That the first parliament had less authority, because but few condescended to it, and that this last parliament of great authority, because more condescended to it? It goes not by the more or lesser part, but by the wiser, truer and godlier part.

'Mercy and justice'

Rogers would have said more but Gardiner interrupted him again and repeated his earlier question, and urged him to answer, for there were more prisoners he wanted to question. Lord William Howard asked Rogers to tell him what he would do: whether he would enter into one church with the whole realm as it was.

Rogers: No, I will first see it proved by the Scriptures. Let me have pen, ink and books, etc. and I shall take upon me so plainly to set forth the matter, so that the contrary shall be proved to be true; and let any man who will, confer with me by writing.

Gardiner: No, that shall not be permitted you. You shall never have so much proffered you as you have now, if you refuse it and will not now condescend and agree to the Catholic Church. Here are two things: mercy and justice. If you refuse the queen's mercy now, then you shall have justice ministered to you.

Rogers: I never offended nor was disobedient to her grace, and yet I will not refuse her mercy. But if this shall be denied me to confer by writing and to try out the truth, then it is not well, but too far out of the way. You yourselves (all the bishops of the realm) brought me to the knowledge of the pretended primacy of the bishop of Rome, when I was a young man twenty years ago, and will you now without conference have me to say and do the contrary? I cannot be so persuaded.

Gardiner: If you will not receive the bishop of Rome to be supreme head of the Catholic Church, then you shall never have her mercy you may be sure. And regarding conferring and trial, I am forbidden by the Scriptures to use any conferring and trial with you. For St Paul teaches me that I shall shun and eschew a heretic after one or two admonitions, knowing that such a one is overthrown and is faulty, in as much as he is condemned by his own judgement.

Rogers: My lord, I deny that I am a heretic: prove that first and then allege your text.

Gardiner, evading Rogers's remark, said: If you will enter into one church with us, tell us that, or else you shall never have so much proffered you again, as you have now.

Rogers: I will find it first in the Scripture and see it tried thereby, before I receive him [the bishop of Rome] to be supreme head.

Strange tongues

Here the bishop of Worcester taunted him by saying he did not understand his Creed, which expressed belief in 'the holy Catholic Church'.

Rogers: I do not find the bishop of Rome in the Creed 'I believe in the holy catholic church', for catholic does not signify the Romish church. It signifies the consent of all true teaching churches of all times and of all ages. But how should the bishop of Rome's church be one of them when it teaches so many doctrines that are plainly and directly against the word of God? Should that bishop be the head of the catholic church who does so? That is not possible.

Gardiner: Show me one of them, one, one, let me hear one [false doctrine].

Rogers: Well said, I will show you one.

Gardiner: Let me hear that.

Rogers: The bishop of Rome and his church say, read and sing all that they do in their congregations in Latin, which is directly and plainly against 1 Corinthians 14.

Gardiner: I deny that, I deny that it is against the word of God. Let me see you prove that. How can you prove that?

Rogers started to quote the beginning of the chapter, saying, 'To speak with tongues is to speak with a strange tongue, as Latin or Greek, etc, and so to speak is not to speak to me but to God. But you speak in Latin, which is a strange tongue, therefore you speak not to men but only to God.' Gardiner granted that they spoke not to men but to God.

Rogers: Well, then it is in vain to men.

Gardiner: No, for one man speaks in one tongue and another in another, and all is well.

Rogers: Nay, I will prove then that he speaks neither to God nor man, but to the wind.

Rogers was intending to declare how these two texts agree, namely, to speak not to men but to God and to speak to the wind; and so to have proved the matter, but there was too much noise and confusion.

Gardiner: To speak to God and not to God were impossible.

Rogers: I will prove them possible.

Lord William Howard said to Gardiner, 'No. Now will I bear you witness that he is out of the way. For he granted first, that they who speak in a strange speech, speak to God; and now he says the contrary, that they speak neither to God, nor to man.'

Rogers turned to Howard and said, 'I have granted or said as you report.

I have alleged the one text and now I am come to the other. They must agree, and I can make them agree. But as for you, you do not understand the matter.'

Howard: I understand so much that that is not possible.

Gardiner then began to tell Howard how when in northern Germany, they all, who had before prayed and used their service all in German, began then to turn part into Latin and part into German. Richard Pates, the bishop of Worcester, then said, 'Yes, and at Wittenberg too.'

The noise was so loud that Rogers could not be heard. He wanted to say, 'Yes, in a university, where men for the most part understand Latin, and yet not all in Latin.'

The Scriptures

He would have gone on to answer Gardiner and to prove his argument, but realizing that the talking and noise were too great, he just thought these comments in his heart, allowing them in the meantime to talk among themselves: 'Alas, neither will these men hear me if I speak, nor yet will they suffer me to write. There is no remedy but to let them alone and commit the matter to God.' Eventually he managed to be heard and said, 'I will make the texts agree and prove my purpose well enough.'

Gardiner: No, no, you can prove nothing by the Scripture. The Scripture is dead: it must have a lively exposition.

Rogers: No, no, the Scripture is alive. But let me go forward with my purpose.

Pates: No, no, all heretics have alleged the Scriptures for them, and therefore we must have a lively expositor for them.

Rogers: Yes, all heretics have alleged the Scriptures for them; but they were confuted by the Scriptures and by no other expositor.

Pates: Yes, but the heretics would not confess that the Scriptures overcame them, I am sure of that.

Rogers: I believe that, and yet were they overcome by them, and in all Councils they were disputed with and overthrown by the Scriptures.

Rogers would have declared how they ought to proceed and to have again come to his purpose, but it was impossible for one asked one thing and another said something else so he was forced to hold his peace and let them talk. Even when he would have proved his argument, Gardiner told him to return to prison. 'Away, away,' said Gardiner, 'we have others to talk with. If he will not be reformed, away, away.' Rogers then stood up, for he had been kneeling all the time.

The queen's mercy

Then Sir Richard Southwell, who stood by in a window, sneeringly intimated to Rogers, 'You will not burn in this gear when it comes to the purpose, I know that,' meaning that if things went wrong for Rogers, he would not be so confident in his beliefs or fearless in the face of death.

Rogers: Sir, I cannot tell, but I trust to my Lord God, yes, lifting up my eyes to heaven.

Thomas Thirlby, the bishop of Ely, then very kindly told Rogers much about the queen's sentiments and intentions, saying that she took them who would not receive the bishop of Rome's supremacy to be unworthy of her mercy. This bishop seems to have been the only person present who treated him with some sort of respect and civility, and Rogers was careful to respond accordingly. It is worthy of note that Thirlby, though always attached to the Church of Rome, was so honest and moderate that he commanded the esteem and admiration of all parties. He invariably treated the Protestants mildly and must be separated from the rest of his class.

Rogers: I would not refuse her mercy, and yet I never offended her in all my life; and that I sought her grace, and the Council, to be good to me, reserving my conscience.

Rogers accused of breaking the law

Many then spoke at once, urged on by Sir John Bourne, one of Mary's principal secretaries, and they accused him of being a married priest and therefore breaking the law.

Rogers, knowing this to be a gratuitous falsehood, replied: I have not broken the queen's law, nor yet any law of the realm, for I married in a country where it was lawful [and he did not return to England until the laws of the realm recognized and justified the marriage of priests].

Rogers could have added that, not only were these marriages generally legalized, but in his own case a special Act of parliament had been passed, making his wife and children citizens and involving his legal recognition in those relations.

They all spoke out at once again, asking, 'Where was that?' thinking it was unlawful everywhere.

Rogers: In Germany. And if you had not here in England made an open law that priests might have wives [referring to the Clergy, Marriage Act passed in 1548, which repealed all previous 'laws, canons, constitutions and ordinances' prohibiting the marriage of ecclesiastics], I would never have come home again; for I brought a wife and eight children with me, which you can be sure I would not have done if the laws of the realm had not permitted it before.

There was a great commotion, with some saying that he had come too soon. One said that there was never a Catholic man or country that ever granted that a priest might have a wife.

Rogers: I said the catholic church never denied marriage to priests, nor yet to any other man.

As Rogers was leaving the room, the prison official, who had brought him, grabbed him by the arm to escort him away. Nicholas Heath, a zealous Catholic but otherwise an amiable man, turned towards him and accused him of not knowing where that church was or is. Rogers, who insisted on having the last word, just managed to reply that he could tell where it was, before the prison official quickly led him through the door. Rogers wanted to give a more complete answer to all the objections and to prove his arguments. He was informed that he would have an opportunity on another day.

Rogers's prayer

He returned to his cell in Newgate, knowing that what he had experienced was but the prelude to other speedy and more decisive proceedings.

When he wrote out his account of these proceedings, which he finished on Sunday 27 January 'at night', he stated that he had just been informed that he was to appear the next morning before some tribunal. He then added the words:

I desire the hearty and unfeigned help of the prayers of all Christ's true members ... of the true unfeigned catholic church, that the Lord God of all consolation will now be my comfort, aid, strength, buckler and shield; as also of all my brethren who are in the same case and distress, that I and they may despise all manner of threats and cruelty, and even the bitter burning fire and the dreadful dart of death, and stick like true soldiers to our dear and loving captain Christ, our only Redeemer and Saviour, and also the only true head of the catholic church, that does all in us, which is the very property of a head (and is a thing that all the bishops of Rome cannot do) and that we do not traitorously run out of his tents, or rather out of the plain field from him, in the most jeopardy of the battle, but that we may persevere in the fight (if he will not otherwise deliver us) till we be most cruelly slain of his enemies.

For this I most heartily, and at this present, with weeping tears most instantly and earnestly desire and beseech you all to pray. And also, if I die, to be good to my poor wife [Adriana], being a stranger, and all my little souls, hers and my children. Whom with all the whole faithful and true catholic church of Christ the Lord of life and death, save, keep and defend, in all the troubles and assaults of this vain world, and to bring at last to everlasting salvation, the true and sure inheritance of all Christians. Amen. Amen.

A farce

The above examination shows that the whole proceeding was a farce, for the Council had already decided on Rogers's condemnation before they examined him. The affair was characterized by unfairness, injustice and falsehood. There was not one accusation that he did not instantly deny or disprove, only to be met by jeers and insults. The Council met, not to determine innocence or guilt, but to transact certain formalities, in order that their next proceedings might appear to be based on some new and positive offence that Rogers had committed. That offence was his refusal to acknowledge the Pope as the supreme head of the church, which by then was a legalized crime. To be actually guilty of the offence, he should have been a free man at the time he committed it.

Gardiner prepares the way

In between Rogers's two examinations, Gardiner was not idle, but took the opportunity to prepare the people for the drastic measures he was about to employ. On Friday 25 January an immense procession passed through the streets of London, headed by Bonner and eight other bishops and 160 priests—probably to represent the same number who, at the late session of parliament, had acknowledged the Pope's supremacy—all dressed in full canonicals. The lord mayor and other city officials were also present, while the cardinal and even King Philip attended during some part of the ceremonies. The shrewd Lord Chancellor knew all too well that such festivities and pomp would stir up the passions of the people to submit to his purposes.

The whole day was passed alternatively in solemn and joyous celebrations, and the night was illuminated by numerous bonfires and other spectacles, and all London, save the prisoners in Newgate, retired to rest, tempted to believe that the new reign was the best the realm had ever known, and thinking little about the men who were about to brighten the sky with another sort of fire.

Rogers's second examination

O n Monday 28 January, Cardinal Reginald Pole, as lord legate of England, issued in general terms his commission for judicial proceedings against all persons who might be obnoxious to the new laws against heresy—a commission that had been prepared before that date. The commission was addressed to Gardiner and other bishops, some of whom would have gladly declined the responsibility if they had dared to resist the mandate of the Pope's representative. The tribunal assembled the same day in the Lady Chapel at the Church of St Mary Overie, chosen probably because of its close proximity to the palace of the bishop of Winchester.

Rogers refuses mercy

Three men were to be examined: Rogers, Hooper and Cardmaker. Gardiner presided, as chief of the commission. Two of these men were the special objects of his hatred and he could not miss the opportunity to condemn them, while the third initially recanted, for which he wanted to take the credit. Bonner, as might be expected, sat at his right hand. Many were present merely as spectators, attracted by the novelty and importance of the occasion, but a few did take part in the proceedings, although not recognized officially as members of the tribunal. Hooper was questioned first, then Cardmaker and lastly Rogers.

Rogers was examined in the afternoon. Gardiner started by asking him the same question he had propounded a week before, whether he would come into one church with the bishops and the whole realm, as was concluded by parliament, and so receive the mercy before offered to him; and whether, with the whole realm, he would come out of the schism and error in which he had long been and recant of his errors.

Rogers: Before I could not tell what your mercy meant, but now I understand that it is a mercy of the antichristian church of Rome, which I utterly refuse, and that the rising which you spoke of, was a very fall into error and false doctrine. I had been and would be able by God's grace to prove that all the doctrine, which I had ever taught, was true and catholic, and that by the Scriptures and the authority of the fathers who lived 400 years after Christ's death.

Gardiner would not grant such a request, for Rogers was a private man and might not be heard against the determination of the whole realm. 'When a parliament has concluded a thing,' Gardiner argued, 'should one, or any private person, have authority to discuss, whether they had done right or wrong? No, that may not be.' Strictly speaking, this was legally and logically correct, but Rogers was not about to move from his position of making his case on the authority of the Scriptures.

Rogers: All the laws of men might not, nor could rule the word of God, but that they all must be discussed and judged thereby, and obeyed; and my conscience, nor no Christian man's, could be satisfied with such laws as disagreed with that word.

Rogers falsely accused

Rogers was willing to continue but Gardiner interrupted him and began a long tale about his answer. He said that there was nothing in the prisoner as to why he should be heard, but ignorance, arrogance, pride and vainglory in even presuming to question the acts of the late parliament.

Rogers granted that his ignorance was greater than he could express, but he was confident, by God's strength and assistance, to be able by writing to perform his word. Nor was he so utterly ignorant as Gardiner would make him, but all was of God, to whom he gave thanks. He was never proud or vainglorious. The entire world knew well to whom the terms pride, arrogance and vainglory were most properly applicable.

Gardiner evaded the personal allusion and accused him of condemning the queen and the whole realm of being of the church of antichrist. Rogers answered that the queen's majesty would have done well enough if it had not been for his counsel.

'The queen went before me,' replied Gardiner, 'and it was her own motion.'

'I neither could nor would ever believe it,' said Rogers. This honest and heartfelt response, uttered at such a time and under such circumstances, ought at least to have saved his life. It was one of the greatest compliments, although misguided, the queen ever received and she should have treasured it.

Then Robert Aldrich, bishop of Carlisle, coming to the relief of Gardiner, said that all the bishops would bear him witness.

'Yes, that I believe well,' replied Rogers, which made the people laugh. (On that day there were many spectators, but on the following day his accusers kept the doors closed to keep out the general public.)

Sir Robert Rochester, Mary's controller of the household, and Sir John Bourne, in defiance of the rules and etiquette of judicial tribunals, both stood up to bear witness. Rogers said little in response, knowing that they were too strong and powerful and would be believed before him—'yes, and before the Saviour Christ and all his prophets and apostles!' Afterwards Rogers recorded his belief that they were equally guilty with Gardiner in forcing the queen's formal consent to their measures. It thus appears that Rogers, right up to his death, regarded the queen more favourably than many others after him, or at least as less guilty than her advisers.

The sacrament

After many words with which Gardiner covered his retreat, he asked Rogers what he meant concerning the sacrament, and as he spoke he stood up and took off his cap (and so did his fellow bishops) in the same way that Henry VIII did when sitting in judgement on John Lambert. He asked whether Rogers 'believed in the sacrament to be *really* and *substantially* the very body and blood of Christ the Saviour who was born of the Virgin Mary and hanged on the cross'.

Rogers replied that he had often told Gardiner that it was a doctrine in which he was no meddler, probably meaning he had not fully made up his mind or that he had been inclined to retain his old opinions concerning it. He certainly had not gone to the extreme opposite position of repudiating the doctrine, as his brethren generally had done and as a result had been subjected to suspicions. He did not hesitate to state his unsettled opinion on the matter.

However, just in case his examiners thought he was about to make further concessions, he said, 'Notwithstanding, even as the most part of your doctrine in other points is false, and the defence thereof only by force and cruelty; so in this matter I think it to be as false as the rest. For I cannot understand the words *really* and *substantially* to signify otherwise than corporally; but corporally Christ is only in heaven, and so Christ cannot be corporally also in your sacrament.'

Rogers accuses Gardiner

Rogers then turned defence into attack with the following charge: 'My Lord, you have dealt with me most cruelly. For you have set me in prison without law and against law, and kept me there now almost a year and a half. For I was almost half a year in my house, where I was obedient to you (God knows) and spoke with no man. And now I have been a full year in Newgate at great cost and charges [the prisoners were compelled to pay for their own provisions], having a wife and ten children to look after, and I had never a penny of my livings, neither of the prebend, nor of the residence, neither of the vicarage of Sepulchre, which was against the law.'

All of these preferments Rogers held at the time of his incarceration and examinations for he had not yet been legally deprived of them. For the past year the income from these livings had been entirely withheld from him, and his family had been ejected from the prebendal residence attached to St Paul's, where he appears to have lived until he was sent to Newgate.

Gardiner's extraordinary response

Gardiner, confused by this sudden and unexpected attack, made another extraordinary declaration. Instead of attempting to defend himself by saying that he had acted under the colour of the queen's or the Council's authority, he blurted out: 'Ridley, who had given these [preferments] to you, was a usurper, and therefore you are the unjust possessor of them.'

Rogers: Was the king then a usurper, who gave Ridley the bishopric?

Gardiner, without realizing the force and effect of this reply, immediately said: 'Yes.' In answering in the affirmative he was virtually denying the rightful supremacy of Queen Mary—whose only claim to the succession lay in the fact that she was Edward's sister—which in effect was little less than treason. As if to justify his remark he began to set out the wrongs that King Edward had done to Bonner, the bishop of London, and to himself. Then, recovering his composure and realizing what he had said and its implications, he admitted that he had misused his terms in calling the king a usurper. Rogers said that 'the word had gone out of the abundance of the heart before', and added that he thought he was not really sorry for what he had said. Rogers was questioning Gardiner's loyalty to the queen, or at least regarding it as secondary to his own personal interests and those of his church.

Gardiner accuses Rogers

Rogers had the good sense to leave the subject at this point and asked, 'Why have you sent me to prison?'

Gardiner: Because you preached against the queen.

Rogers: That is not so, and I would be bound to prove and to stand the trial of the law, that no man should be able to prove it, and thereupon would set my life. I preached a sermon at Paul's Cross, after the queen went to the Tower, but said nothing against the queen. I call the large audience as my witness. You, after my examination, had let me go free after the preaching of that sermon.

Gardiner: Yes, but you did read your lecture against the commandment of the Council.

Rogers: I did not. Let that be proved and let me die for it. Thus have you now against the law of God and man handled me, and never sent for me, never conferred with me, never spoke of any learning until now that you have got a whip to whip me with [Rogers is referring to the statutes of Richard II, Henry IV, and Henry V, affecting heretics, which were revived by Mary] and a sword to cut off my neck, if I will not condescend to your mind. This charity does all the world understand.

Gardiner remained silent, as he knew he had uttered a falsehood, but he would not allow Rogers to say any more. Rogers records that if he had been allowed to speak further, he would have said that it had been time enough to take away men's livings and to imprison them after they had broken the law; for they are good citizens that break no laws and worthy of praise and not punishment. But their purpose was to keep him in prison so long, until they might catch him in their laws and so kill him. He could and would have added the example of Daniel, who by a craftily devised law was cast into the lions' den.

He would have reminded Gardiner of how he had sent two supplications to him from Newgate and how his pregnant wife had many times gone to him, but he had ignored her petitions. He would have mentioned the late and worthy John Gosnold, who had attempted to save him from burning, and how many other men took trouble in the matter. 'These things,' he said to Gardiner, 'declare your antichristian charity, that you seek my blood and the destruction of my poor wife and my ten children.'

John Cardmaker

He would also have referred to the defection of his fellow-prisoner John Cardmaker. Cardmaker (*alias* Taylor) had been vicar of St Bride's, Fleet Street, and then prebendary and chancellor of Wells. When the persecution broke out under Mary he made a vain attempt to escape overseas. He was caught and thrown into the Fleet, where he remained until his examination, when it was understood he recanted.

According to Rogers, Cardmaker made a complete submission and a promise to recant. He 'forsook us,' said Rogers, 'and stood not to his tackle, but shrank from under the banner of our master and captain Christ; the Lord grant him to return and fight with us, till we be smitten down together, if the Lord's will be so to permit it; for yet shall not a hair of our heads perish against his will, but with his will. The same Lord grant us to be obedient to the end and in the end. Amen. Sweet, mighty and merciful Lord Jesus, the Son of David and of God, Amen, let every true Christian say and pray.'

Cardmaker was remanded to the Counter in Bread Street, with the prospect of a speedy deliverance. Afterwards, in a letter to a friend, Cardmaker declared that he merely temporised with the bishops, in order to secure a little delay for a particular purpose, the motive for which should shortly appear and be 'satisfactory to his friends'; but it did not appear.

It has been presumed that later, through the influence of Laurence Saunders, one of his fellow prisoners, Cardmaker changed his mind, for he was again arraigned on 25 May 1555 and condemned for heresy. Five days later, on coming to the stake with his fellow prisoner, an upholsterer by the name of Warne, the sheriffs called him aside and talked with him secretly. The people were greatly concerned, thinking that Cardmaker would recant if he had to witness the burning of Warne. At length Cardmaker left the sheriffs and approached the stake, knelt down, and made a long prayer in silence to himself. He then stood up, took off his clothes to his shirt and went with a bold courage to the stake and kissed it; and taking Warne by the hand, he heartily comforted him, and was bound to the stake, rejoicing. The people seeing this so suddenly done, contrary to their previous expectation, cried out, 'God be praised! The Lord strengthen thee, Cardmaker! The Lord Jesus receive thy spirit!' These words of encouragement and supplication continued while the executioner set fire to the faggots, and both men passed through the flames to that blessed rest and peace of God's holy saints and martyrs.

The examination ends

The time was about four o'clock and Gardiner said that he and the church must yet use charity with Rogers, who characterized such 'charity' as similar to that of foxes and wolves towards chickens and lambs. He was given until the following day to see whether he would return to the Catholic Church again and repent; and if he did, they would receive him mercifully.

Rogers, with some appearance of indignation, said: I was never out of the true catholic church, nor ever would be; but into your church would I, by God's grace, never come.

Gardiner: Well then, is our church false and antichristian?

Rogers: Yes!

Gardiner: And what is the doctrine of the sacrament?

Rogers: False!

Rogers then made some gesture, which one of the bystanders, in an abortive attempt at wit, said was that of a player, an insult Rogers treated with the contempt it deserved.

Gardiner: Come again tomorrow morning between nine and ten.

Rogers: I am ready to come again, whenever you call.

Rogers taken back to prison

The officers then took hold of him and led him out onto the street to take him to the Compter in Southwark. Down to the year 1541, the parishes of St Margaret and St Mary Magdalen adjoined each other, but were that year united by an Act of parliament under the name of St Saviour. The old parish church of St Margaret was built during the twelfth century and stood on the site nearby known as St Margaret's Hill. Along with its graveyard it was sold to the authorities and converted into an assize or sessions house, one portion of it being used as a prison and called the Compter in Southwark. It was in the immediate vicinity of St Mary Overie's church.

Hooper went before Rogers, and there was such a great crowd of people that they had difficulty walking in the streets. Hooper, who had gone into the street first, stopped for a moment and when Rogers appeared, said to him, 'Come, brother Rogers, must we two take this matter first in hand, and begin to fry these faggots?'

'Yes, sir,' replied Rogers, 'by God's grace.'

'Doubt not,' returned Hooper, 'but God will give us strength.'

In this brief but important communication between these two men, both made a solemn pledge not to deny their faith, but to depend on God's strength right to the end.

The martyrdom of John Cardmaker and John Warne

Rogers's third examination

On Tuesday 29 January both Rogers and Hooper were sent for in the morning, about nine o'clock, and fetched by the officers from the Compter in Southwark and taken to the church of St Mary Overie. After Hooper had been condemned they called for Rogers. The crowd was not admitted and no one was allowed in except those known to be Gardiner's servants and adherents. Gardiner did not want to undermine his own authority as he had done the day before and he did not think it advisable to let any Protestant sympathizers hear and then report publicly the sarcastic but truthful language of the bold rebel with whom he was dealing.

George Day

George Day, the bishop of Chichester, seems to have acted officially for the remainder of the trial. At one time Day had been sympathetic to the Reformation. In the convocation of 1542 he had been appointed as one of the doctors to translate part of the New Testament, in the abortive attempt of the clergy to have a really authorized version of the Scriptures, which was quashed by King Henry. The following year he was consecrated bishop of Chichester and joined with Cranmer in an effort to abolish superstitious ceremonies. During Edward VI's reign he was part of the celebrated Windsor Commission, which drew up the first English order of communion and the first English Prayer Book.

However, he grew more 'Catholicical', and for preaching against the illegal destruction of altars by the Council he was thrown in the Fleet and deprived the following year. He was released when Mary entered London in 1553 and restored to his see before the end of her first year. It is said of him that in 1555 he visited Bradford in the Compter and during a long conversation confessed to the prisoner that 'though as a young man, fresh from the university, he had complied with the first steps of the Reformation, it had always been against his conscience'. He certainly took part in the persecutions in his diocese and personally sentenced a number of Protestants to be burned. He died on 2 August 1556.

Rogers's defence

It had been decided to deal with the prisoners hastily at this day's session and so Gardiner wasted no time with his leading question.

Gardiner: Rogers, here you were yesterday and we gave you liberty to remember yourself this night whether you would come to the holy Catholic Church of Christ again or not. Tell us now what you have determined, whether you will be repentant and sorry, and will return and take mercy again?

Rogers did not answer that question at once: My lord, I have remembered myself right well what you yesterday laid for you, and desire you to give me leave to declare my mind what I have to say; and that done, I shall answer your demanded question. When yesterday I desired that I might be suffered by the Scripture and authority of the first, best and purest church to defend my doctrine by writing, meaning all the doctrine I have ever preached, you answered me that it might not, nor ought not to be granted me, for I was a private man; and that the parliament was above the authority of all private persons, and might not have the sentence thereof found faulty by me being but a private person. And yet, my lord, I am able to show two examples that a man has come into a general Council, after the whole Council had determined and agreed on an act or article, and has, by the word of God, declared so clearly that the Council had erred in decreeing the said article, that he caused the whole Council to alter and change the act or article they had before determined.

Rogers referred to Augustine (whose opinion on any other occasion would have been regarded as conclusive), who, when disputing with a heretic, said that he would have the Scriptures to be their judge rather than two former Councils; and to a lawyer, who said that to a simple layman, who brings the word of God with him, there ought to be given more credit than to a whole Council gathered together without the Scriptures.

Rogers continued: These things well prove that I ought not to be denied to say my mind and to be heard against a whole parliament, bringing the word of God for me and the authority of the old church 400 years after Christ, albeit that every man in the parliament had willingly and without respect of fear and favour agreed thereto (which thing I doubted not a little of), especially seeing that the like had been permitted in the old church, even in general Councils; yes, and that in one of the chiefest Councils that ever was, to which neither any of the acts of parliament, for the most part, nor yet any of the late general Councils of the bishops of Rome, ought to be compared.

Sir Anthony Browne, who recently had been raised to the peerage by the title of Viscount Montague, a fact of which Rogers was unaware, interrupted him before he could allege the example of the Act that made the queen a bastard and the king the supreme head of the church. 'Then will you,' said Rogers sarcastically, pointing to Gardiner, 'and you and you and so you all,' pointing to the rest of the bishops, 'say "Amen": yes, and it please your grace, it is meet that it be so enacted.'

However, Rogers did manage to tell his judges that if Henry VIII were alive and should call a parliament to re-enact the old laws, they would, even then, be found to be his most obsequious servants and flatterers, regardless of the zeal they were now showing for the new laws.

Gardiner the bully

At this point Gardiner would not allow him to speak anymore and told him mockingly to sit down, saying that he was sent for to be instructed by them and not to be their instructor.

Rogers: My lord, I stand and sit not. Shall I not be suffered to speak for my life?

Gardiner: Shall we suffer you to tell a tale and to prate?

With that Gardiner stood up and began to 'bully' Rogers in an arrogant, proud fashion, for he realized that the prisoner had in some way 'touched' him, which he thought to hinder by putting a stop to his argument, and so he did; for Rogers was not allowed to return to his argument again, not even one word of it. Then Gardiner had a similar communication with him as he had had the day before, as his manner was, 'taunt for taunt, and check for check'. Rogers told him, being God's cause, he should not make him afraid to speak.

Gardiner: See what a spirit this fellow has, finding fault with my accustomed earnestness and hearty manner of speaking.

Rogers: I have a true spirit, agreeing and obeying the word of God.

He wanted to say that he was 'never the worse, but the better to be earnest in a true, just cause and in his master Christ's matters', but he was not to be heard, for Gardiner was more interested in reading the sentence of condemnation against his enemy than in listening to his 'pointless prattle'. The end for Rogers was very near.

Condemned

G ardiner proceeded to the excommunication and condemnation of Rogers after the latter had told him that his church of Rome was the church of antichrist; meaning, the false doctrine and tyrannical laws, maintained by the cruel persecution used by the bishops of that church, of which the bishop of Winchester and the rest of his fellow bishops in England were the chief members.

Similarly, when Rogers was accused of denying the sacrament, he asked Gardiner—who took off his cap, more to maintain his authority than from any true reverence of a Christian institution—after what order he spoke of it, for the *manner* of the bishop's speaking did not agree with his words. Gardiner was not happy and asked the audience whether Rogers had not simply denied the sacrament. They agreed with him, for most of them were his own servants. Rogers replied that he would never deny that he had stated that Gardiner's doctrine of the sacrament was false.

Gardiner reads the sentence of condemnation

Gardiner then read the official sentence of condemnation against Rogers, the man whom he had hated for eighteen years. The sentence was in the general form adopted for such occasions, the language being slightly varied to suit each respective case, and was based on that which had been pronounced on Joan of Kent a few years before. It embraced two particular charges: that Rogers affirmed the Romish Catholic Church to be the church of antichrist, and that he denied the real presence of Christ in the sacrament. On these two charges alone Rogers was condemned.

The condemnation, which highlights Gardiner's hypocrisy and deviousness, read in part as follows:

In the name of God, Amen. We, Stephen, by the permission of God, bishop of Winchester, lawfully and rightly proceeding with all godly favour, by authority and virtue of our office, against you, John Rogers, priest, *alias* called Matthew, before us personally here present, being accused and detected and notoriously slandered of heresy; having heard, seen and understood, and with all diligent deliberation weighed, discussed and considered the merits of the cause; all things being observed, which by us in your behalf, in order of law, ought to be observed, sitting in our judgement seat, the name of Christ being first called on, and having only God before our eyes; because, by the acts enacted, propounded and exhibited in this matter, and by your own confession judicially made before us, we do find that you have taught, held and affirmed, and obstinately defended other errors, heresies and damnable opinions, contrary to the doctrine and determination of the holy church, as namely these: *that the Catholic Church of Rome is the church of antichrist; and that in the sacrament of the altar, there is not, substantially nor really, the natural body and blood of Christ.* The which aforesaid heresies and damnable opinions being contrary to the law of God, and determination of the universal and apostolical church, you have arrogantly, stubbornly and wittingly maintained, held and affirmed, and also defended before us, as well in your judgement, as also otherwise, and with the like obstinacy, stubbornness, malice and blindness of heart, both wittingly and willingly have affirmed that you will believe, maintain and hold, affirm and declare the same...

We have gone about oftentimes to correct you, and by all lawful means that we could, and all wholesome admonitions that we did know, to reduce you again to the true faith and unity of the universal Catholic Church; notwithstanding have found you obstinate and stiff-necked, willingly continuing in your damnable opinions and heresies, and refusing to return again to the true faith and unity of the holy mother church, and as the child of wickedness and darkness so to have hardened your heart, that you will not understand the voice of your shepherd, which with a fatherly affection does seek after you, nor will not be allured with his fatherly and godly admonitions; we therefore ... not willing that you who are wicked should now become more wicked and infect the Lord's flock with your heresy (which we are greatly afraid of) with sorrow of mind and bitterness of heart do judge you and definitively condemn you the said John Rogers ... as guilty of most detestable heresies, and as an obstinate impenitent sinner, refusing penitently to return to the lap and unity of the holy mother church, and that you have been and are by law excommunicated, and do pronounce and declare you to be an excommunicated person.

Also we pronounce and declare you being a heretic to be cast out from the church and left to the judgement of the secular power, and now presently so do leave you as an obstinate heretic and a person wrapped in the sentence of the great curse, to be degraded worthily for your demerits.

The 'great curse'

The sentence nominally only excommunicated him from the Roman Catholic Church and delivered him into the hands of the secular authorities for further proceedings, but in reality it placed him under what was known as the 'great curse' of that church, the consequences of which were that anyone having the slightest communication with him, or eating and drinking in his company or giving him anything, became subject to the same penalties. It also doomed him, without further ceremony, to the tortures of death by burning.

'I stand before God'

Rogers knew very well that every prospect of life had melted away with the condemnation and that it was only a matter of a few days, maybe even a few hours, before he was called to face that fiery ordeal; yet he remained unmoved. After the sentence was read, he said,

Well, my lord, here I stand before God and you, and all this honourable audience, and take him to witness, that I never wittingly or willingly taught any false doctrine; and therefore have I a good conscience before God and before all good men. I am not afraid, but I shall come before a judge that is righteous, before whom I shall be as good a man as you; and I do not doubt but that I shall be found there a true member of the true catholic church of Christ and everlastingly saved. And as for your false church, you need not excommunicate me from it. I have not been in it these twenty years, the Lord be praised.

These were among the last words of a man who was about to be burned at the stake, and his honesty and determination to stand up for the truth are apparent for all to witness. He then humbled himself to ask one favour of his heartless judge, 'But now you have done what you can, my lord, I pray you yet grant me one thing.'

'What is that?' responded Gardiner hurriedly, perhaps hoping that Rogers wanted time to consider his recantation; but in this he was quickly disappointed, for Rogers was not thinking of himself but of those he loved.

Rogers: That my poor wife being a stranger, may come and speak with me so long as I live. For she has ten children that are hers and mine, and I would counsel her what were best for her to do.

Gardiner, with not a shred of compassion, responded: No, she is not your wife.

Rogers: Yes, my lord, and has been these eighteen years.

Gardiner: Should I grant her to be your wife?

Rogers: Choose you whether you will or not; she shall be so nevertheless.

Gardiner then shouted: She shall not come to you.

Rogers: Then I have tried out all your charity. You make yourselves highly displeased with the matrimony of priests, but you maintain open whoredom, as in Wales, where every priest has his whore openly dwelling with him and lying by him, even as your holy father suffers all the priests in Germany and in France to do the same.

Gardiner, knowing the truth of what had just been said, did not answer, but seemed to squint. He then handed his enemy over to the officials. Rogers departed and did not see him again. It has been stated that Gardiner never afterwards appeared as a judge at the trials of the Protestants. As he presided in person at Rogers's trial, it is further evidence of the bitter and personal malignity that he entertained against his foe.

The official record

The account of Rogers's judges, which they placed on record, reads as follows:

Monday, 28 January 1555. On the day and at the place aforesaid the said John Rogers, *alias* Matthew, was produced for trial; whom my lord addressed and exhorted that he should reconcile himself and return to the unity of the Catholic Church. But he, with a shameless mind and forward spirit, presently burst out into some such words as these: 'My lord, where you say you willed me to rise again with you, and so to come to the unity of Christ's church, I take you, by those your words, that you willed me to fall; for I do understand the church otherwise than you do: for I do understand the church of

Christ, and you do understand the Romish Church of antichrist: and I say that the Pope's church which you believe is the church of antichrist.'

Also he said, as touching his belief in the sacrament of the altar, that he believes that Christ is in heaven, and believes not that his very body and blood are really and substantially in the sacrament of the altar.

Also he said that, in that he, being a priest, did marry, he offended no law.

And said also, that the bishops maintain herein one false faith, one false doctrine, and one false word.

The premises being transacted, my lord appointed the same John Rogers to make appearance the next day, in this place, between eight and ten o'clock in the morning, to attend on further proceedings.

On which day, Tuesday, 29 January, in the place aforesaid and before the said reverend father, the bishop of Winchester, with the bishops, his colleagues, who are specified above in the before written acts of this day, and in the presence of us, the aforesaid notaries, the said John Rogers, *alias* Matthew, again appeared; whom the lord bishop of Winchester pressed to recant, with many reasons, arguments, persuasions and exhortations: notwithstanding and utterly scorning which, Rogers persisted stubbornly in his perverse mind. And then, the lord bishop, proceeding against him as an obstinate and stubborn heretic, pronounced a definite sentence of condemnation, and delivered him over to the secular court, and committed him to the said sheriffs of London, who took him away.

On the production of whose sentence, the said reverend father required us, the undersigned notaries, &c.

Present, then and there, they to whom reference has been made in the before written acts of this day.

The charges of the official record roughly agree with what Rogers had said in his own account, thus underlining the real character of his alleged offences.

His last days

The authorities were worried that an attempt would be made to rescue Rogers and Hooper on the evening of their condemnation. News of the trial and sentence had leaked out and no doubt there were some who were not prepared to accept the merciless destruction of two good men.

Returned to prison

In order to safeguard the prisoners on their journey from the judgement hall in St Mary Overie's Church to their old quarters in Newgate, they were first moved to the Clink in Southwark, where they remained until night. The Clink was a small prison on the Bankside, so called because it was the prison of the Clink Library or manor of Southwark, which belonged to the bishop of Winchester. It was used mainly for holding disorderly persons and other petty offenders. It stood at the corner of Maid Lane and was abandoned about 1745, having become unsafe from decay.

Orders were then given to extinguish the lights in the street through which the prisoners were to pass, including the torches on the stalls of the costermongers, with officers sent out in advance to make sure the orders were carried out. The intention was that the prisoners and their attendants would pass over the route without being recognized or interrupted.

When all the arrangements had been put in place and secrecy secured, Rogers and Hooper, who had no thought of attempting to escape, were taken from the Clink under a heavy guard of officers armed with 'bills and weapons enough'. They were first led through the bishop's house, a magnificent palace, to mislead the bystanders, then through St Mary Overie's churchyard and into the open streets, across London Bridge towards Newgate. The precautions for privacy were in vain, for the officers found, to their surprise and annoyance, that the streets were lined with men and women holding lighted candles in their hands and cheering the prisoners as they passed by, giving affectionate greetings and assurances of sympathy, as well as thanksgiving for their courage and prayers for endurance. This was the only way these people had of showing their respect and feelings and they could not be restrained. This demonstration was not serious and so the authorities took no subsequent notice of it.

Rogers re-entered his cell that night at Newgate knowing that his days were few, although no notice was given to him as to the precise day of his execution.

During the next five days his confinement was rigid and solitary and no one made any further attempt to persuade him to recant, probably realizing that it was a hopeless task. Bradford and others wrote many letters and sent messages to their friends at this time, but not a word or line of a letter or note has been passed down from Rogers, probably indicating the severity and rigidity of his imprisonment. Rogers was left on his own to reflect on his fate and that of his unhappy family.

What he *would* have said

However, he did manage to elude the watching jailers and write out an account of his examinations and what he *would* have said at his hearings if Gardiner had permitted it. Some of the arguments it contained are: his support for the marriage of priests; a spirited defence of the Protestant preachers against the charge that they were disturbers of the realm; how it was lawful for a private man to reason and write against a wicked act of parliament or an ungodly counsel; and an attempt to prove that prosperity was not always a token of God's love (that is, he replied to Gardiner's assertion that the accession of Mary to the throne demonstrated that Catholicism was the true religion). He made this latter point because Gardiner boasted about himself that he had been delivered from prison miraculously and preserved by God to restore true religion to the realm and to punish Rogers and other heretics like him. From the closing paragraph it appears that he was not able to finish, ending abruptly for lack of time, with his last prayer and final blessing: 'God's peace be with you. Amen.' These are appropriate words from one who had been so instrumental in translating the Bible, from whose inspirations, under the blessing of the Holy Spirit, God's peace is derived.

John Day

During the last few days of his life he did manage to hold a conversation with a fellow prisoner John Day, a 'zealous reformer', who had been imprisoned for setting up a secret press and printing Protestant polemical works under the name of Michael Wood. After his release Day became one of the most successful printers and publishers of his times, producing about 230 works, many of importance. Apart from the first English edition of Foxe's *Acts and Monuments*, he issued many other works concerning the Reformation. He also published several editions of the Bible with Rogers's notes. He went abroad for a time, but resumed his business on his return and seems to have continued it until his death on 23 July 1584.

John Day

Although the prisoners were not allowed to talk to anyone from outside the prison, there were brief moments when they could converse with each other. According to Day, Rogers said to him, 'You shall live to see the alteration of this religion and the Gospel to be freely preached again; therefore, have me commended to my brethren, as well as those in exile as others, and bid them be circumspect in displacing the Catholics and putting good ministers into the churches, or else their end will be worse than ours.'

Rogers knew that Day would soon be released and he wanted him to communicate the results of his own experience to his Protestant brethren, particularly to those in exile who would return when the present dynasty was overthrown, which Rogers believed would not be long. He wanted to warn them to avoid the fatal errors, which had led to such distressing results in the true church during Edward's reign. He urged them to replace all Catholic priests with Protestant ministers. The failure to do so in Edward's reign had led to serious problems for the Reformation on the accession of the new sovereign; for Catholics far outnumbered Protestant clergy even at Edward's death and retained an overwhelming influence over the people, which became absolute as soon as a change in government united the civil and religious powers.

A system for when the persecution ends

Rogers also communicated to Day that when the present persecutions should cease, there would be a lack of educated and reliable Protestant ministers from among those whose lives had been spared. Therefore, superintendents should be chosen, each of whom should be in charge of ten churches or congregations, having under him faithful and competent readers or assistants, who should act like curates and for whose character and conduct he should be responsible. At least once a year the superintendent should visit officially each parish, examine carefully the conduct of its minister and his effect on the congregation and either confirm him in his position or replace him with a better man. In this way every church throughout the realm might be supplied without retaining a single Catholic priest. The bishops of each diocese should exercise the same authority and supervision over the superintendents and hold them to a strict yearly account.

Rogers's system was only designed to be temporary and the various churches were to be supplied with regular clergymen as soon as they became qualified to assume more responsible positions. Hooper seems to have approved and recommended this course of action and it was somewhat adopted after the accession of Elizabeth I.

It was actually followed by congregations that maintained their existence and held their assemblies in London through the persecuting reign of Mary. Austin Bernher, the friend and servant of Latimer and correspondent of Ridley and other martyrs, was one of their preachers. These little bands represented the true Church of England at this troublesome time.

His last days

Rogers seems to have kept both firmness and kindness in his disposition, as well as his cheerfulness during the last days of his life. He agreed with his friends to eat only one meal a day, while the other meal should be given to those prisoners on the other side of the prison who did not have enough. But when the keeper of the prison, Alexander Andrew, 'a straight man and a right Alexander—a coppersmith indeed', found out he put a stop to such liberality. Only the day before his death, being a Sunday, Rogers drank to

Hooper's health, who was housed beneath him, and asked to be commended to him and to tell him that there was 'never a better little fellow, who would stick to a man than he would stick to him'. Rogers thought they were going to be burned together, although it happened otherwise, for Rogers was burned alone. Hooper was taken to Gloucestershire, where he was burned on 9 February 1555. The 'little fellow' may be a reference to Rogers's own stature.

Rogers lay down that last night and committed his soul into the hands of his Saviour. On Monday morning 4 February 1555, the keeper's wife at Newgate, Mrs Alexander Andrew, came to warn him solemnly to prepare himself for the fire. She found him asleep and could hardly wake him by shaking. At last he awoke and was urged to hurry. Being told that his last hour had come, he quietly and coolly replied, 'If it be so, I need not tie my points!' It seems that without even being permitted his usual morning refreshment he was hurriedly dragged to Bonner, who was waiting for him.

The martyrdom of John Hooper

On to Smithfield

Rogers was led down first to Bonner to be degraded from the priesthood. It is a little strange that this humiliation was necessary. Rogers had not professed to be in the Catholic Church for some twenty years and had, during that time, been its ardent enemy; and he had already been formally excommunicated. It was probably a ceremony invariably performed to increase the effect of the punishment on the people, although it was pointless. Rogers was arrayed in the full canonicals of the office he bore, although he had not worn these garments for years, and then they were torn from him piecemeal, accompanied with certain prescribed invocations and anathemas.

As soon as the last curse had been uttered, Rogers asked Bonner for one favour. 'What is that?' asked Bonner.

'Only that I may talk a *few words* with my wife before my burning.' In all probability Rogers wanted to tell his wife about the book of examinations and answers he had written, which he had secretly hidden in a corner of the prison, but predictably Bonner refused permission.

David Woodruff

Bonner was supported by several of his confidential officers and servants and a large number of guards. Between ten and eleven o'clock Rogers was handed over to two officers, William Chester and David Woodruff, then officials of London, whose responsibility it was to carry out the executions in Smithfield. Woodruff was a most willing instrument of the law on this and other occasions and has been described as a 'most cruel and heartless character'. While the kind-hearted Chester wept at the death of the martyrs, Woodruff would laugh and beat the condemned. Soon after the death of Bradford, whom he had taunted and whose hands he had ordered to be tied when he refused to stop praying, Woodruff was struck with paralysis and had to be bedridden for more than seven years. He was buried on 31 March 1563.

Instead of allowing Rogers time to commune with God, Woodruff approached him and asked if he would revoke his abominable doctrine and his evil opinion of the sacrament of the altar. Rogers, who was not going to recant at this late stage, answered emphatically, 'That which I have preached, I will seal with my blood.'

Woodruff: You are a heretic.

Rogers: That shall be known at the day of judgement.

Woodruff: Well, I will never pray for you.

Rogers was unperturbed and graciously replied: But I will pray for you.

Woodruff was silenced and proceeded with his duties.

On to Smithfield

For the last time Rogers was hurried through the gate of the dreary prison that had been his home for more than twelve months, and amid a formidable array of armed guards was led towards Smithfield. He may have gazed back, giving one long last look at the cathedral where he had often ministered and breathed a silent prayer for those within its precincts. A few steps further on and he was brought within the shadow of his own church walls, and maybe then the bell of St Sepulchre, which had often called him to its altar, was chiming a funeral dirge for its pastor. Thousands of spectators lined the route and he would have recognized many a face. The guards, by whom he was surrounded, could not stop the cries of joy and sorrow—sorrow that their friend and teacher was about to be torn from them in such a cruel manner, and joy that he marched to the stake so triumphantly.

Rogers quoted Psalm 51, which was traditionally recited by the condemned at their executions. Many stood amazed at his constancy and gave great praises and thanks to God, while even the enemies of his faith described him and the scene as like a bridegroom going to meet his bride at the wedding altar. Count Noailles, then the French ambassador at London and a zealous Catholic, wrote to Montmorency on the same day,

This day was performed the confirmation of the alliance between the Pope and this kingdom, by a public and solemn sacrifice of a preaching doctor named Rogers, who has been burned alive for being a Lutheran; but he died persisting in his opinion. At this conduct, the greatest part of the people took such pleasure, that they were not afraid to make him many exclamations to strengthen his courage. Even his children assisted at it, comforting him in such a manner that it seemed as if he had been led to a wedding.

His wife of eighteen years and eleven children, ten able to stand and the other leaning against Adriana's breast, met him by the way as he went towards Smithfield. Their anxious faces were all fixed on him and their voices of pain reached his ears. Since 27 January 1554, when he was taken to Newgate, he had not seen or received any news of his family, so this was the first and last time he saw his new baby, which had been born during his imprisonment. The sorrowful sight of his own flesh and blood did not weaken his determination, but he faced death with wonderful patience and in the defence of Christ's gospel.

The spectators were more numerous than on any subsequent occasion and although he was not permitted to say much, he did exhort them to remain true to the faith and doctrine he had taught them. He told them he was not only content to suffer and bear all such bitterness and cruelty as had been shown him for the sake of the truth, but also would most gladly resign up his life and give his flesh to the consuming fire for the testimony of Christ.

Burned at the stake

After he had been bound to the stake but before the faggots were set ablaze, his pardon, in official form, was brought and presented to him if he would recant, but he utterly refused it on those terms. In all probability his acceptance of it would not have saved his life, but it would have been at the expense of everything he held dear. All that he had taught and the life he had lived would have been destroyed and the effect produced on the people would have inflicted a sharp blow to the vitality of the Reformation.

So in the presence of Sir Robert Rochester and Sir Richard Southwell, the two official witnesses from the Court, and a large crowd, the fire was lit. As it engulfed both his legs and shoulders, he washed his hands in the flames as if they were tongues of cold water, metaphorically ridding himself of the last impurities of earth. After lifting up his hands to heaven, not lowering them until such time as the devouring fire had consumed them, he yielded his spirit to his heavenly Father and entered his eternal reward.

According to Susan Brigden in *London and the Reformation* Rogers suffered 'with heroic fortitude. Even catholic opponents said so. The godly who had gathered wept and prayed God to give him courage to bear the

The martyrdom of John Rogers

pain and not to recant … some seeing birds fly over as he expired thought this a sign of the Holy Ghost.'

The day after his execution Simon Renard, Charles V's ambassador, wrote to King Philip and expressed his concern at the public reaction to Rogers's martyrdom and at the same time gave further details of the tragic scene: 'Sir, the people of this town of London are murmuring about the cruel enforcement of the recent Acts of Parliament on heresy, which has now begun, as was shown publicly when a certain Rogers was burned yesterday. Some of the onlookers wept, others prayed to God to give him strength, perseverance and patience to bear the pain and not to recant, others gathered the ashes and bones and wrapped them up in paper to preserve them, yet others threatening the bishops.'

Rogers was the first martyr who suffered in the reign of Mary I, and his courage and constancy at the stake provided a glorious example to all who trod the same fiery path. He is to be placed among the great proto-martyrs and with them he offers perennial encouragement to suffering believers in every land and generation who stand ready to walk through the fires of persecution and to seal their faith with their blood.

Supposed site of John Rogers's martyrdom

The exact spot

The exact spot where Rogers died has been identified. For a long time a square piece of pavement composed of dark coloured stones, a few paces in front of the entrance gate of the church of St Bartholomew-the-Great, traditionally marked the site. In 1849, during excavation work, this pavement was removed and three feet beneath it was found some rough stones and ashes, in the middle of which were a few charred and partially destroyed bones. This spot agrees exactly with the one shown in old engravings of those times.

Two poems

Several poems were written about the life and death of Rogers, two verses of which are worth quoting. The first example by John Taylor was published in *Book of Martyrs* in 1639:

'No sooner Edward was laid in his tomb,
But England was the slaughterhouse of Rome:
Gardiner and Bonner were from prison turned,
And whom they pleas'd were either save'd or burn'd:
Queen Mary, imitating Jezebel,
Advanc'd again the ministers of hell:
Then tyranny began to tyrannize—
Tortures and torments then they did devise:
Then Master Rogers, with a faith most fervent,
Was burn'd and died (in Smithfield) God's true servant.'

The second poem, taken from *The History of the Lives of those famous English Divines that were most zealous in promoting the Reformation* (1709), was written by Nathaniel Crouch, a famous bookseller. His sketch of Rogers's life is prefaced by these lines:

'When good King Edward died, and Popery,
With superstition and idolatry,
Return'd again to plague this wretched nation,
And take away the right means of salvation;
Then Rogers, by the rage of Rome and hell,
A sacrifice to true religion fell.
He did contemn the fury of all those,
Who to the Word of God were mortal foes;
And was the first in bloody Mary's reign
Who lost his life, 'cause he did truth maintain.'

And then …

During Rogers's time in prison a search had been made of his cell and all his letters and writings must have been confiscated by the authorities; yet after his death, his wife and one of his sons, Daniel, went to the place where he had been incarcerated in Newgate to look for his books and writings. They searched for some time but found nothing. Just as they were about to leave, Daniel looked to one side to examine a black 'thing' lying in a dark corner under a pair of stairs. He called to his mother to come and see what it was he had discovered and together they found a book written in John's own hand, containing his examinations and answers.

A prophetic warning
It also contained a prophetic warning to the church, which began:

If God look not mercifully on England, the seeds of utter destruction are sown in it already, by these hypocritical tyrants and antichristian prelates, Popish Catholics and double traitors to their natural country. And yet they speak of mercy, of blessing, of the catholic church, of unity, of power, and strengthening to the realm. This double dissimulation will show itself one day when the plague comes, which will undoubtedly light on these crown shorn captains, and that shortly, whatever the godly and the poor realm suffer in the meanwhile by God's sufferance and will…

For God cannot and undoubtedly will not suffer for ever their abominable lying, false doctrine, their hypocrisy, blood thirst, whoredom, idleness, their pestilent life pampered in all kinds of pleasure; their boasting, pride, their malicious, envious and poisonous stomachs, which they bear towards his poor and miserable Christians… Some shall have their punishment here in this world and in the world to come, and they that do escape in this world, shall not escape everlasting damnation. This shall be your sauce, O wicked Catholics, make merry here as long as you may.

The effect
The burning of Rogers in Smithfield immediately alerted the populace to similar atrocities that were about to be carried out by the authorities. No

one knew who was going to be the next victim or how many victims there were going to be. Those living in apparent security had no idea if they were to be dragged without warning from their families to a speedy trial and summary execution. A sense of dread filled the hearts of those who still clung to their Bibles and practised the Protestant faith. However, the way Rogers went to his death must have emboldened them, for there were few defections on the part of those who professed the Reformed religion.

Letters

When the other condemned preachers in prison heard the news of Rogers's courage and cheerfulness they were moved to lift their hearts to God in praise and thanksgiving. Now they had an example to imitate when their hour came. Bradford, writing to Cranmer, Ridley and Latimer, four days after Rogers's execution, rejoiced that their 'dear brother' had 'broken the ice valiantly'.

Ridley himself wrote to Austin Bernher on 10 February: 'I bless God with all my heart, in his manifold merciful gifts given to our dear brethren in Christ, especially to our brother Rogers, whom it pleased him to set forth first, no doubt but of his gracious goodness and fatherly favour towards him... I trust to God it shall please him, of his goodness, to strengthen me to make up the trinity [i.e. Rogers, Bradford and himself] out of Paul's Church, to suffer for Christ.' Ridley also wrote to Bradford: 'I thank our Lord God and heavenly Father by Christ that, since I heard of our dear brother Rogers's departing, and stout confession of Christ and his truth even to the death, blessed be God! So rejoiced of it, that, since that time, I say, I never felt any lumpish heaviness in my heart, as I grant I have felt sometimes before.'

This frank admission of weakness by Ridley and the strengthening effect that Rogers's martyrdom had on him, underlines the importance attached to that sobering event by his fellow sufferers and the place of eminence that Rogers deserves for being the first in Mary's reign to be put to death for his faith.

John Leaf

John Leaf, a citizen's apprentice, only nineteen years of age, was arrested by the authorities because of his youthful zeal towards the truth of God and subjected to several examinations by Bonner, during which he resisted every inducement and threat that could be brought to bear on him, and maintained, although unable to read or write, strong arguments against the doctrines of his judges. He was finally thrown into prison, where it was thought he could be more easily worked on and two papers were brought to him, one containing a full recantation and the other a recapitulation of the professions he had made at his public trial.

After listening to the first one, he utterly refused to sign his mark to it; but on hearing the other paper, he seized a pin, thrust it into his hand and sprinkled his blood over the paper, asking those present to witness his sign-manual. He was then asked if he had been one of John Rogers's scholars, to which he promptly replied that he had been and that he not only firmly believed all the doctrines he had been taught by him, but was ready to meet the same death as his old master had already endured in defence of the same faith. According to his desire, he was burned, with Bradford, and showed a cheerfulness and an unshaken resolution that were remarkable for one so young and that would have pleased his teacher in the faith.

Coverdale's marriage

An interesting fact is that Rogers may well have been the indirect means of saving Coverdale's life. What made Rogers particularly obnoxious was the fact that he was a married priest, which increased the bitterness already against him. Coverdale, on the other hand, unlike Rogers, had been an Augustinian friar before his marriage and had taken the vows of celibacy. The sister of Coverdale's wife had married John Macalpine, who was highly favoured by the king of Denmark. At Macalpine's urgent request, the king was induced to intercede with Queen Mary that Coverdale, then under house arrest in Exeter, might be allowed to leave England. At first the queen refused, but on a further demand she did not think it advisable to refuse for a second time one whom she desired to keep as a powerful ally; and so Coverdale and his wife escaped to Denmark before the end of the month in which Rogers was executed. Had it not appeared from the developments in Rogers's trial that his marriage constituted an additional and weighty offence, and therefore Coverdale was under threat on that account, it is possible that the Danish king would not have exerted his influence so readily and effectively on his behalf.

Rogers's family

There is no account of the immediate movements of Rogers's family after his execution, and no news of Adriana following her final visit to the prison, probably on the day of her husband's death. It is possible they all returned to Germany together, for Daniel Rogers received part of his education at Wittenberg, their former residence. However, a few years after their father's death, at least six of the children were settled in England.

In a manuscript in the British Museum, Rogers's children are listed as follows: Daniel of Sunbury, county of Middlesex; John, a proctor of the civil law; Ambrose; Samuel; Philip; Bernard; Augustine; Barnaby; Susan; Elizabeth and Hester.

Daniel Rogers was educated partly abroad and partly at Oxford, where he was admitted BA on 18 July 1561 and licensed to proceed in the same faculty on 1 August. He married Susan, the daughter of Nicasius Yetswiert, clerk of the signet and secretary for the French tongue, and became one of the clerks of the Council in the reign of Elizabeth, who repeatedly employed him in embassies abroad. He was regarded as a 'very good man, an excellent scholar and a most accomplished gentleman of his time'. It is not unreasonable to suppose that Melanchthon, a warm personal friend of his father, assumed the care of Daniel at Wittenberg for sometime subsequent to Rogers's death. In a letter that the historian John Foxe wrote to Daniel, he encouraged 'the most beloved of his friends' by alluding to the example of his father, 'Go on, then, O my Rogers, in the virtue which you would seem to have derived (or imbibed), not from the books of the philosophers, but from *the paternal imprint.*'

There is little noteworthy information concerning Rogers's other children.

May the God of all grace inspire us to walk in the footsteps of John Rogers and to imitate his determination to witness for Christ; may he encourage us to stand up for the truth regardless of the opposition we might face; and embolden us to live out our Christian lives without compromise or fear, even in the midst of many dangers. Our great enemy, that wily serpent, the devil, will use all the weapons in his armoury to entice us from the faith and boldness of the Reformers and to ensnare us in the trap of double mindedness. May we resist all the temptations he lays before us to disgrace the Captain of our salvation, either by our silence or our sin, and to bear on our lips and in our hearts the great confession of the first Marian martyr: 'That which I have preached, I will seal with my blood.'

Opposite: Martyr's memorial at Smithfield, the rear of St Bartholomew's Hospital
The text reads:

BLESSED ARE THE DEAD WHICH DIE IN THE LORD.

THE NOBLE ARMY OF MARTYRS PRAISE THEE.

WITHIN A FEW FEET OF THIS SPOT
JOHN ROGERS,
JOHN BRADFORD,
JOHN PHILPOT,
AND OTHER
SERVANTS OF GOD,
SUFFERED DEATH BY FIRE
FOR THE FAITH OF CHRIST
IN THE YEARS 1555, 1556, 1557.

NEAR THIS PLACE A CHURCH
IS ERECTED
TO THE MEMORY
OF THE SAID MARTYRS.

The Smithfield Martyrs' Memorial Church,
St John Street Road, London

Martyrs' Memorial at Oxford, near the site of the burning of
Thomas Cranmer, Hugh Latimer and Nicholas Ridley

Select bibliography

Anderson, Christopher, *The Annals of the English Bible* (2 vols) (London: William Pickering, 1845).

Brigden, Susan, *London and the Reformation* (Oxford: Clarendon, 1989).

Brown, Andrew J., *Robert Ferrar: Yorkshire Monk, Reformation Bishop, and Martyr in Wales (c.1500–1555)* (London: Inscriptor Imprints, 1997).

Burnet, Gilbert, *The History of the Reformation of the Church of England* (1829).

Chester, Joseph Lemuel, *John Rogers: The Compiler of the First Authorised English Bible* (London: Longman & Co., 1861).

Colvile, Frederick Leigh, *The Worthies of Warwickshire who lived between 1500 and 1800* (Warwick: H. T. Cooke & Son, 1870).

Cooper, Charles Henry, *Athenae Cantabrigienses* (vol.1) (Cambridge: Deighton Bell, 1858–1861).

Cotton, Henry, *Editors of the Bible* (Oxford: University Press, 1852).

Coxon, Francis, *Christian Worthies* (Zoar Publications, 1980).

Crouch, Nathaniel, *The History of the Lives of those famous English Divines that were most zealous in promoting the Reformation* (London: 1709).

Daniell, David, *The Bible in English* (London: Yale University Press, 2003).

Daniell, David, *William Tyndale: A Biography* (London: Yale University Press, 1994).

D'Aubigné, J. Merle, *History of the Reformation of the Sixteenth Century* (Rapidan: Hartland Publications, n.d.).

Dictionary of National Biography (22 vols) (London: Oxford University Press, 1959–1960).

Edwards, Brian H., *God's Outlaw* (Darlington: Evangelical Press, 1993).

Elton, G. R., *England under the Tudors* (London: Methuen & Co Ltd, 1969).

Foxe, John, *Foxe's Book of Martyrs* (http://www.hrionline.ac.uk/foxe/index.html, 1583).

Lewis, John, *A Complete History of the Several Translations of the Holy Bible and New Testament into English* (London: H. Woodfall, 1739).

Loane, Marcus, *Masters of the English Reformation* (Edinburgh: Banner of Truth Trust, 2005).

MacCulloch, Diarmaid, *Thomas Cranmer* (London: Yale University Press, 1996).

Maitland, Samuel Roffey, *Essays on Subjects Connected with the Reformation in England* (London: Rivington, 1849).

McGrath, Alister, *In the Beginning* (London: Hodder & Stoughton, 2002).

Mozley, James Frederic, *Coverdale and his Bibles* (London: Lutterworth Press, 1953).

Newcourt, Richard, *Repertorium Ecclesiasticum Parochiale Londinense* (London: 1708–10).

Oliver, W. Robert, *The Marian Martyrs* (Evangelical Times, March 2005).

Peirce, James, *A Vindication of the Dissenters* (London: 1717).

Phillips, W., *John Rogers, the Birmingham Martyr* (n.d.).

Rex, Richard, *The Tudors* (Stroud: Tempus, 2005).

Ridley, Nicholas, *Works* (Parker Society, 1841).

Routh, C. R. N., *Who's Who in Tudor England* (London: Shepheard-Walwyn, 1990).

Ryle, J. C., *Light from Old Times* (Welwyn: Evangelical Press, 1980).

Strype, John, *Annals of the Reign of Queen Mary,* in *England: A Complete History of England,* vol. 2 (1706).

Strype, John, *Ecclesiastical Memorials* (Oxford: Clarendon Press, 1822).

Strype, John, *Memorials of the Most Reverend Father in God Thomas Cranmer* (Oxford: 1812).

Taylor, John, *Book of Martyrs* (London: 1639).

Weinreb, Ben & Hibbert, Christopher, *The London Encyclopaedia* (London: Papermac, 1993).

Wood, Anthony A., *Athenae Oxonienses* (London: 1813–20).